CW00525722

Redlands

Philip Brookman

... for those who sleep in dust.

Redlands

Philip Brookman

Steidl

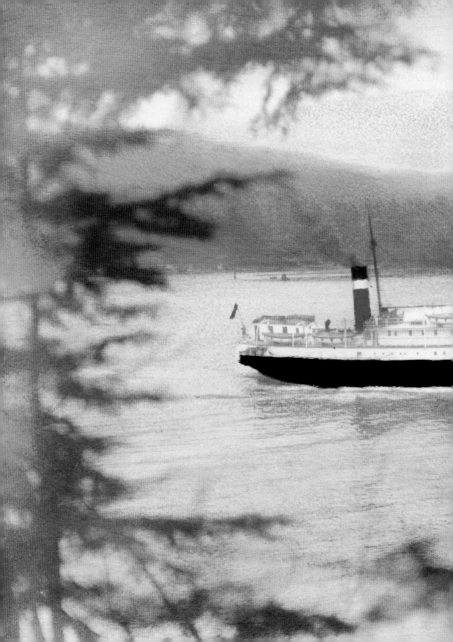

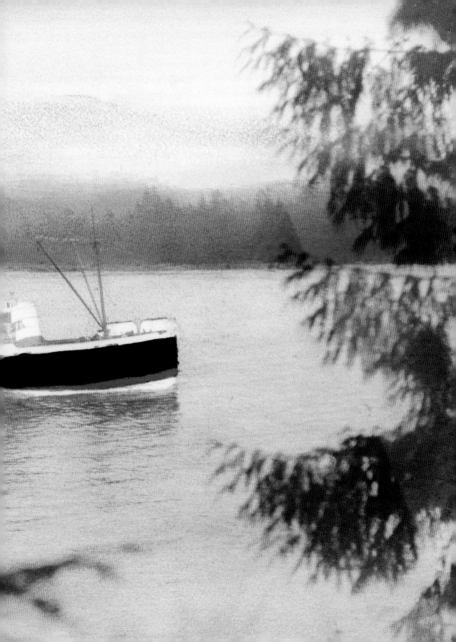

Leo (July 23-Aug. 22)
Though nothing earth-shattering seems to be going on, take photographs anyhow. This helps you recall what happened today, which will be far more remarkable in the light of memory.

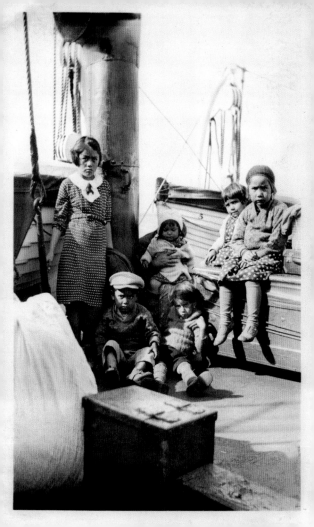

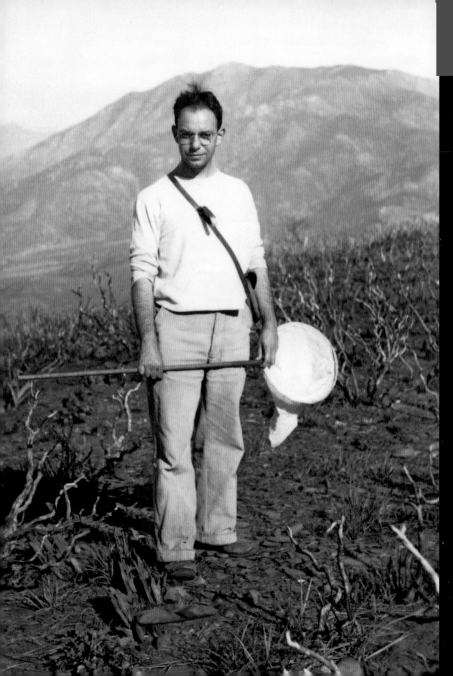

Redlands, California, 1948

They first got to know each other while working up in the scrub foothills out of Oaxaca, which today sounds pretty romantic but it wasn't.

He was out there casting about for an idea after abruptly deciding to drop out of Stanford. He had a little money saved from a season on the farm at Marshall, directly across Tomales Bay from home. But he couldn't tolerate the cows in Marin—they made him nervous—and after the war he couldn't stand to be at school, it just made no sense to him. This was three years after getting back from a twenty-four month detour to Europe; "It was a giant freezing gray fucking shithole," was all he would say about that experience. "Everything was dead or dying." He didn't have to kill anybody but he'd had his fill of it anyway. And he wouldn't make that a personal thing; he put it all in a concrete box in his mind and wrapped it up tight in chains. Then he hustled a semi-adventurous job covering research on bubonic plague for a nature magazine, ending up in Mexico more than a mile above sea level on assignment for an article that paid 10 cents a word.

She was a biologist working on an MS at Cal, struggling to gain acceptance in a profession that didn't respect women doing fieldwork. She always had an easy time with school and never let the academics stand in her way. She was smart and very focused (a perfectionist) and aspired to be the bold scientist who would "rid the world of disease." She had carried this seemingly unattainable ambition on her back since losing her mother in a flu epidemic when she was a baby, just after the first war. Now, three years after the second, she made herself a promise; she would break that invisible thread of discrimination in science that she knew was holding her back. She felt vindicated when she won a competitive fellowship that placed her on a research team headed to Oaxaca.

They met in a cafeteria near the tiny lab, not far from Templo de Santa Domingo de Guzmán. Both had arrived from California, both speaking English and struggling to excise the demons of childhood, both on different but intersecting missions. She agreed to an interview about the "carriers" of plague (monkeys and squirrels) and then drove him to an observation site where spotters were collecting data, counting all the critters in a one-hectare quadrant. Always pretty awkward, she tripped getting out of the car and fell down a ravine, cutting her leg so badly that she immediately had to be flown back to Berkeley. Sorry to see her go, he finished his story (it was technical at best) and caught up with her months later back in San Francisco at a favorite café on Judah. He liked how she looked, always a bit rumpled and spaced, with a beautiful smile he would memorize and never forget.

They were married almost a year later under flowering bougainvillea arches at Rosarito Beach south of Tijuana, and stopped for dinner in Redlands on the drive northwest to Palm Springs for their honeymoon. Redlands was just citrus groves and boxcars back then, with fewer than 20,000 residents and camps for the itinerant workers who came through to harvest and pack the fruit. "It's so dusty here. Wouldn't this be a good hideout for Farley Granger and Cathy O'Donnell in *They Live By Night*?" she asked, imagining a Hollywood reference might impress him. High on clean air and the majesty of the moment, they talked through the night about the beautiful mountains rising out of the desert around Redlands, a landscape that reminded them both of the Sierra Madre, where they had met. "Wouldn't this be a lovely place to bring up children?" she asked, full of questions and the optimism that came with her newfound freedom.

Their friends called them Dave and Jess (or Jack and Jill when they were all joking around; they finished each other's sentences and were so close that some people thought they acted more like brother and sister). When she was barely old enough to talk, my sister Addie called them momma and dada. When I came along I called them something else, but to this day no one remembers what it was.

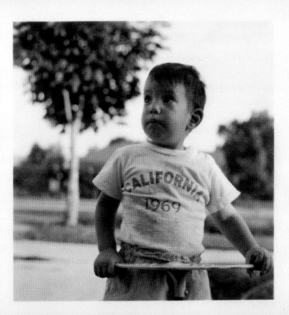

THRU SOME OLD CARDS
LL BE SENDING YOU
...ME DIFFERS — FOR
TE OLD STAMPS an
ITEM — MAYBE YOU'LL
IKE THEM — GOT YOU

Maurice Norman,

THE BEL-AIR
MOTEL

Nags Head Beach, N. C.

Located on U. S. 158, 5.8 miles South Currituck Bridge. Rooms—Efficiency Apts., 2 Bedroom cottages, ocean front, screened porches, Swimming Pool, Television.

For Reservations, Write or call

BEL-AIR MOTEL
Kill Devil Hills, N. C.
Phone 8057

Mom + Dad.

Box 493, Clinton, N. C.

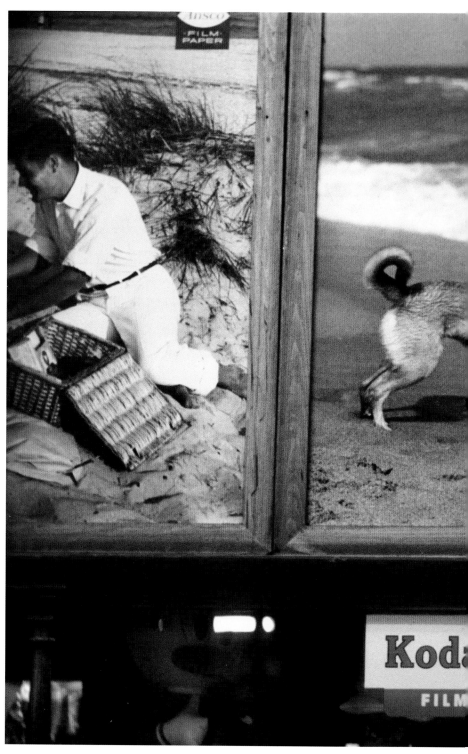

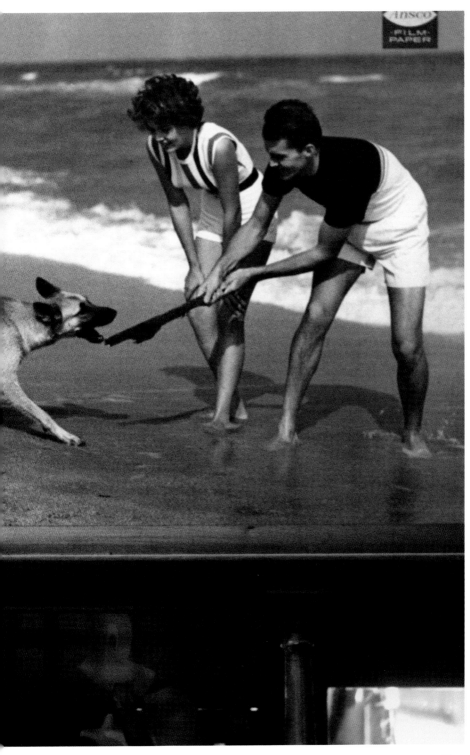

Mexico City, 1962

At least the road was paved. This was one of the few improvements to Colonia Moctezuma that my friend's family had noticed in many years. I remember Calle Emilio Carranza as a dusty cut through the old neighborhood that ran out toward the airport. People loved to walk their dogs on the shaded sidewalks, and you definitely had to watch your step heading out in rubber *huaraches* with a sword and plastic helmet, playing the conquistador riding into battle on a horse. Named for a flyer who became famous in 1928 for piloting a plane cross country from San Diego to Mexico City, Calle Carranza became my first serious memory, a smoggy playground that opened my eyes and led me on a straight path to the world beyond.

Dust got into everything; it covered my skin and clothes, gave my toy guns and dinosaurs an even umber coat, and even got into the grooves of the blues and country albums my dad brought with him to Mexico from the small town of Tomales, where he was born. We tore through the alleys like pirates, jumping the flimsy, corrugated walls put up to protect people's privacy. The air smelled like *maiz frito* as vendors prepared tacos for the day workers and planes propellered in for a landing not far upwind of our street. Dad told me we were here to get away from the past, but at the skinny age of nine I didn't understand what that meant. Then I could only live in the present; the past was a fantasy of volcanoes and leaky sailing ships from picture books, fighting monsters and exploring the uncharted sea.

One day after school I was out hunting ghosts with my friend Juanito when we stumbled on a violent laughter. Following the rising screams, we climbed a mound of loose dirt, dropped down on our bellies, and watched from a distance through make believe binoculars as a mob of boys—they were a bit older than us and dressed for school—taunted a tall *indio* girl they had ambushed. She lay sprawled on her back, scared, fallen, kicking to get away with her legs and arms flailing. I recognized Ramona from school. The air was charged, about to explode; their senseless shouts of "*labios negros, labios negros, negros, negros, negros*" echoed off the neighborhood walls to stifle my mind. "Do people really behave this way?" I asked Juanito in a whispered tone. As he nodded, confirming my innocence, Ramona's black eyes caught mine as the boys started throwing gobs of adobe mud from the construction site, covering her printed linen dress in wet brown goo. She gave up her struggle to escape and simply started sobbing. With a stealth understanding of the danger, Juanito took my arm and we backed away. "Let's go, Kip," he whispered.

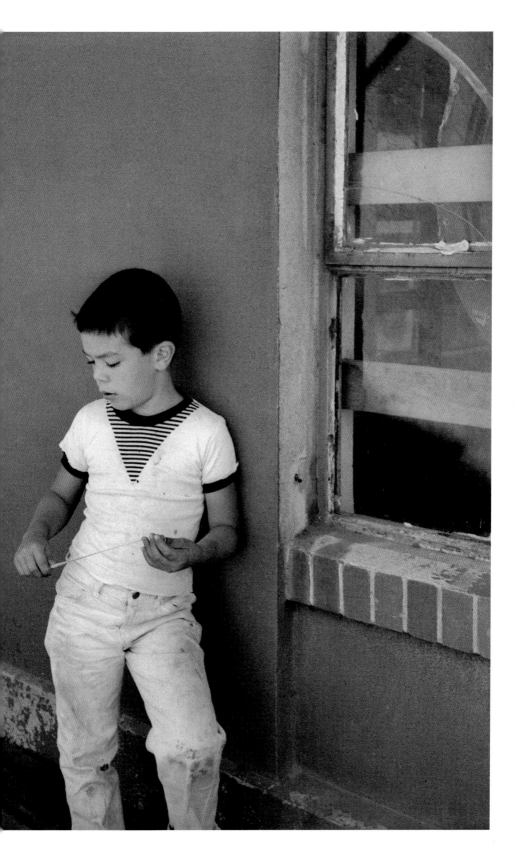

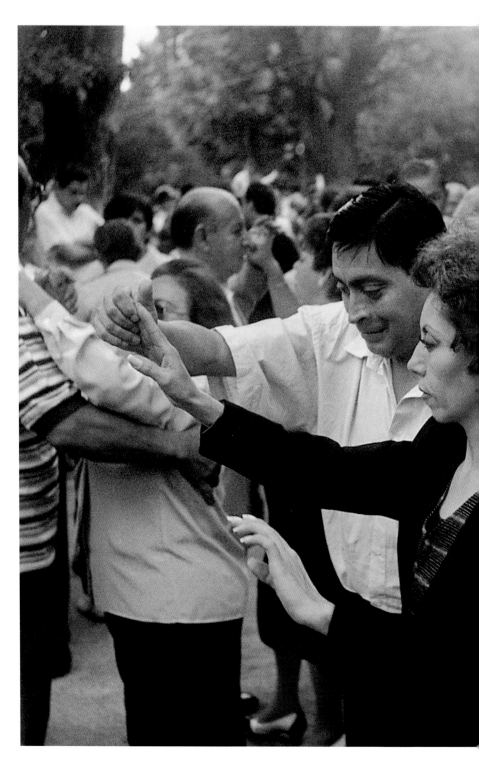

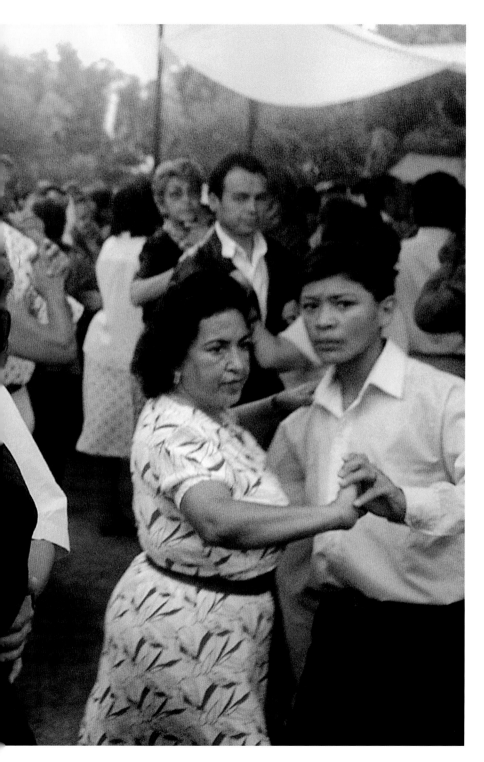

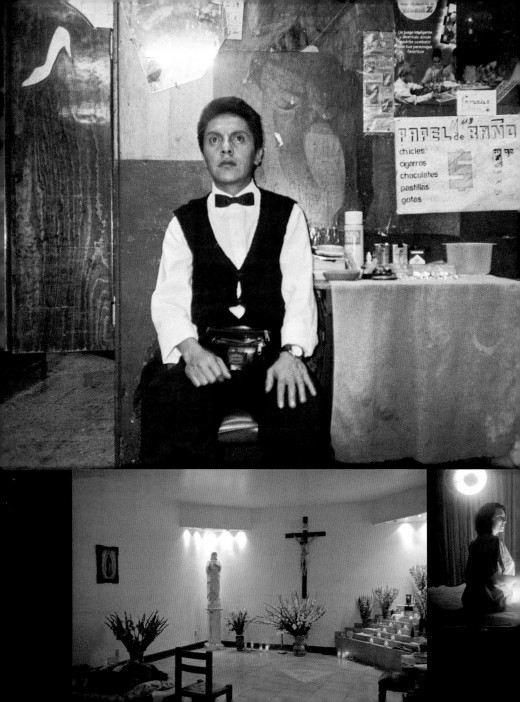

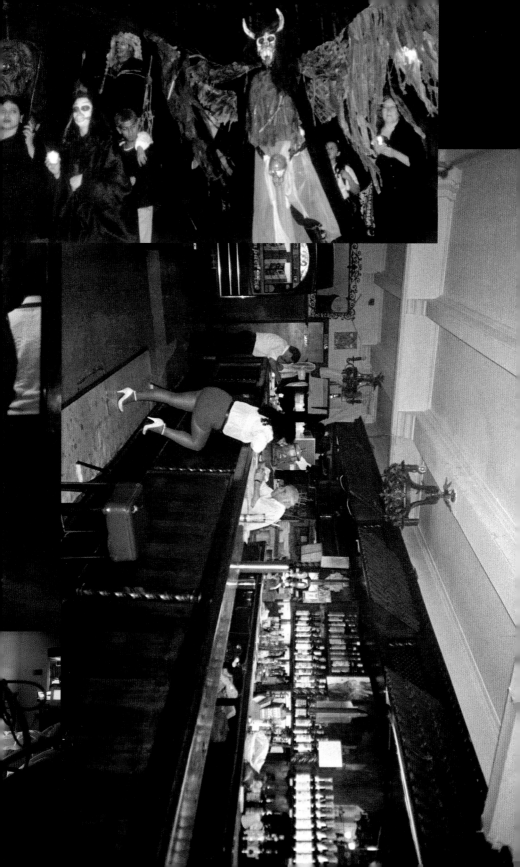

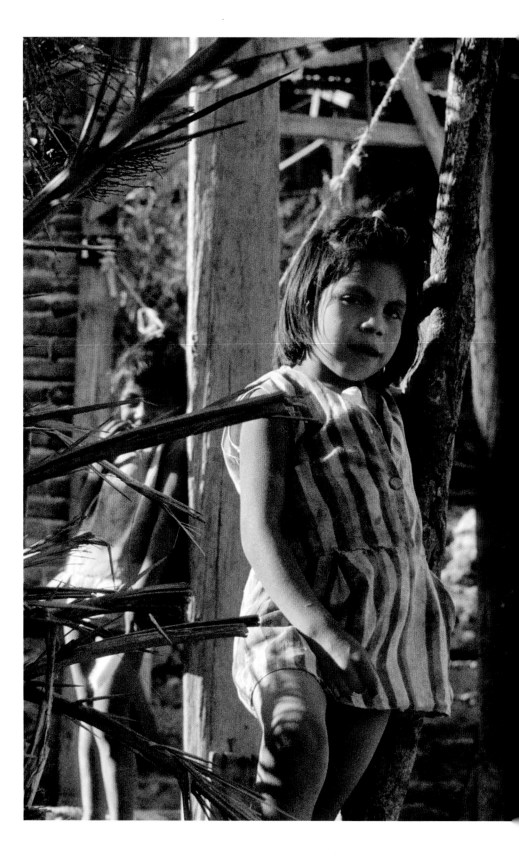

Silence.

As we turned and ran, out of breath and afraid to look back at the attackers, Juanito started yelling, "*Alto…Alto…Alto….*"

Two months later, my dad got a call from home. Mr. Carrillo—the baker downstairs who loved to listen to Dad's Leadbelly albums through the open window—brought him the telegram. My mother had been diagnosed with some sort of cancer and her health was pretty fragile. Right then, Dad decided to leave Mexico and packed us back up north to California. "So you can see her again," he explained when I asked why we had to go.

I still remember the sweet smell of the early morning *pan dulce* in the air as we left our home in Mexico. Driving east out Emilio Carranza to the airport in an old Ford taxi blowing brown smoke into thin blue air, I turned around to survey the old neighborhood. The streets were empty, cool, and very quiet so early on a Sunday morning. The sun was up just enough to color the gray sidewalks with a faint glow of pink, like a naked bulb on a dimmer just coming to life. The light was twinkling a bit as it began to catch on the edges of things. A dog crossed the street, sniffing the air for scraps from last night's dinner. Everything shimmered when the sun warmed the moisture in the air just enough to condense on the cold glass, which dulled the view out the back window. As the taxi slowed at a stop sign, I caught sight of a boy moving quickly in the shadow of an apartment building.

It could have been Juanito, out before dawn to earn an extra peso for his family by sweeping the street. He was focused on cleaning the pavement with a straw broom that was longer than he was tall, and he pulled a small wagon behind him to carry any trash that he could sell. The fine dust stirred by his deliberate strokes solidified the shafts of sunlight sifting through the trees. As the taxi gained distance, we looked through each other, the magic cast by the light receding into memory.

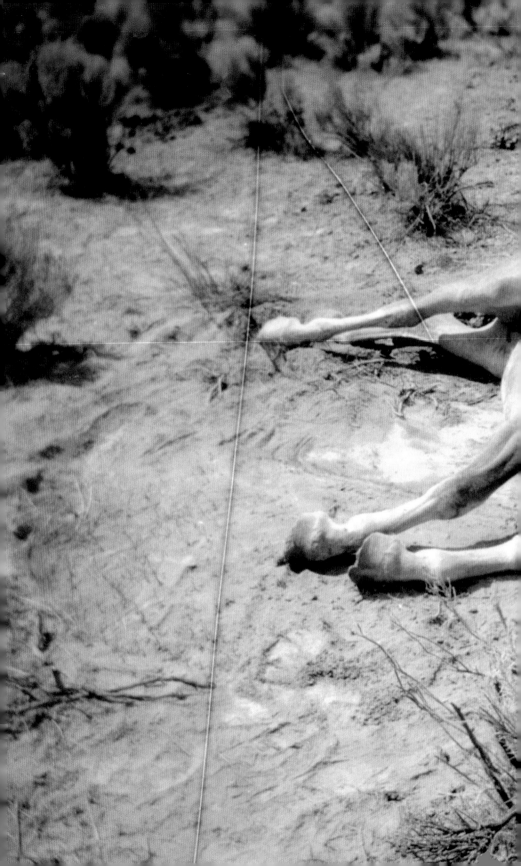

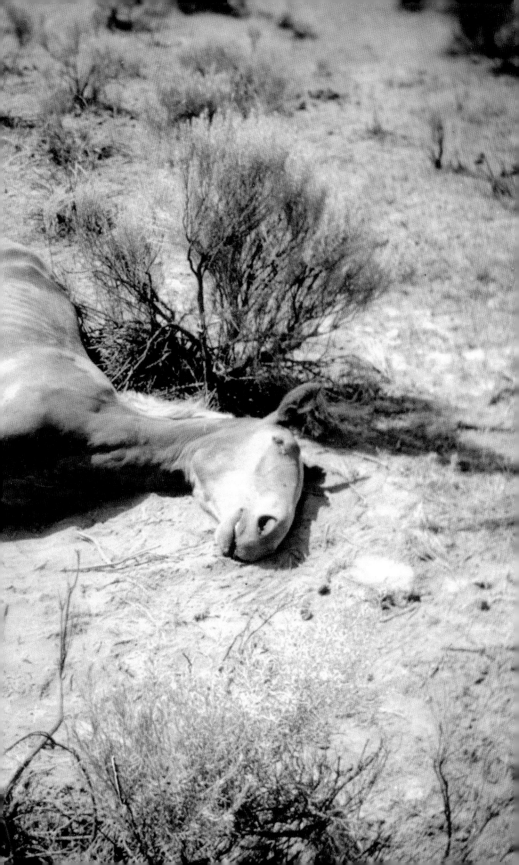

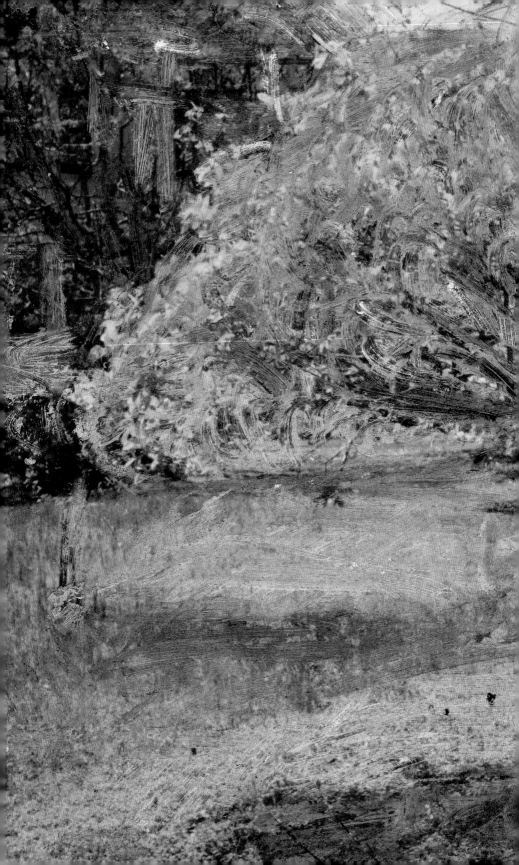

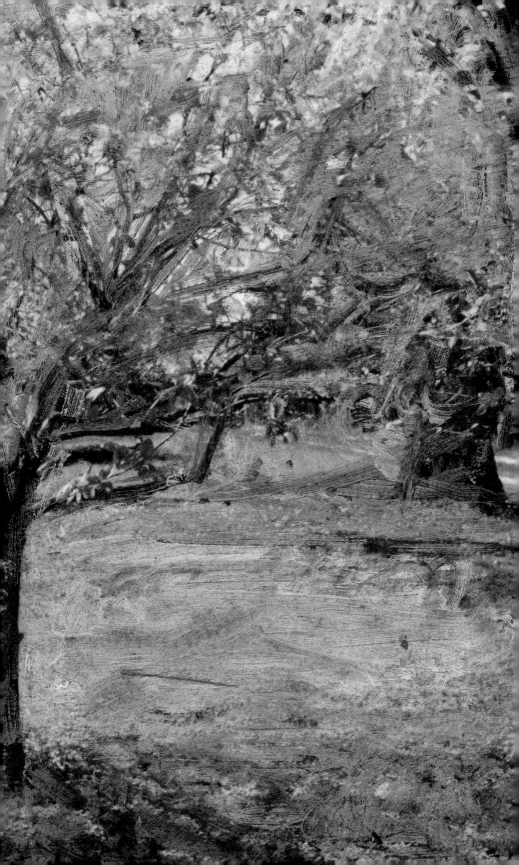

Redlands, California, 1965

As a kid, I thought there were people out there I could trust but I soon learned better of it. After my return from Mexico, it took a while for me to lose my way and find it again, running wayward and free from my favorite booth at the International House of Pancakes, just off the highway exit for Redlands. The booth had a big picture window. I liked this one best ever since my dad and I stopped here the first time we drove to Mexico City. I sometimes thought that after we left Mexico he decided to settle in Redlands just because he liked the view out this window, which looked across a totally bland parking lot onto the Interstate. Plus Redlands was smack in between the ocean and the desert, a place he used to gather inspiration to work again. I liked to sit there with him, to watch and listen to the truckers coming down the off ramp and in for breakfast on a fast run east out of L.A., a brief stop before heading up into Coachella and out across the high desert toward Phoenix. As far as I knew, the only thing beyond that was Mexico, since that was as far as I'd been.

We came in here all the time after he moved us to Redlands in 1964. He was a writer who needed a place to work, a hideout that was rootless and solid at the same time. What he wrote came mostly from his memories, so he didn't have to be in New York City to spin a good story. All he needed was a quiet room and a typewriter, but I needed a stable home after those years away and my mom's cancer. Then she died.

I hated it at first—Redlands is absolutely the most boring place—but once I made a few friends and my sister joined us from Tomales, I took to wandering the railroad tracks and it just lit up my spirit. I started to think about what was out there beyond the pancake place. The name of every town around us sounded like it came from a John Wayne western: Rialto, Calimesa, Roubidoux, and Lugonia were Spanish and Mexican names from the old haciendas that dotted the hills before Americans from back east took over and the railroads rolled through. I thought I was lucky, happy to be back in California and reunited with Addie, but I missed the hazy light and noise of Mexico City and I missed Mom the most.

When the weather was warm (which was all the time) we would ride our bikes out to the Southern Pacific tracks by the packing plants and lie down in the weeds, stealing time to look at the sky and listen to the trains rumbling through town. When the sun got low we rode home and sat in the yard listening over and over to *Bustin' Surfboards*, a not very new album by a local band called the Tornadoes. They were pretty much the only real thing that ever came from Redlands. Their cover of "Summertime" became our new anthem of rebel living, and when the Tornadoes played the Redlands Bowl that summer, Addie was right up front dancing like crazy with some older kids from the neighborhood, her dark brown hair glowing and bouncing in that bad surf-twang da-da-da-da-da-da sort of beat. Our lives were in the music that summer and the music grew inside us.

We decided that we had to go to Malibu to learn to surf, or at least experience the scene for ourselves, to make it real. But I got the feeling that Addie, who was now fifteen—a big three years older than me—was looking up to the older guys. She was seduced by a feeling of freedom in the songs, by the hypnotic frequency of endless waves that undercut their chunky rhythm. So we left home one day in August, telling Dad we were going camping up in the San Bernardino hills, and headed west for L.A., hitching a ride with a trucker who believed we were traveling to meet our uncle, who was, we told him, a Hollywood producer. It didn't make any sense, but Addie and I sat up in the cab, high over the road, listening to the hum of the wheels on wide pavement.

Addie lived with Mom after our parents split up. She was ten and I was seven. That's when Dad took me with him to Mexico City, where he went to get away and write. Addie stayed in Tomales, up the coast from San Francisco through the rainbow tunnel, a tiny town of a few hundred people (mostly dropouts) in west Marin. It's set by the water, smack in between a steep hill and the San Andreas Fault. People say that their fences, homes, animals, and even their lives will be split in two when there's a good shake, one half heading north and the other south. There was evidence for that all around us, much of it left over from the 1906 disaster that almost changed the name of San Francisco to Atlantis.

Dad wanted to travel and he couldn't stand to be disturbed when he was working. Mom said she had no idea who he really was but she loved him still, even if he did change character depending on what he was writing and the color of his drinks. She wanted to go back to school to study medicine but felt stuck in place by two kids, a husband, a drafty house, and a cat named Rouge, in that order. She pampered the cat and wanted stability for herself, a steady life different than the one she'd had as a child. That's the life they made together—by mutual disagreement—until he left her behind to live the dream of bohemian writer in Mexico. But his dream dissolved into the same endless and boring stream of magazine stories he had been writing all along. And then she got sick. Fuck.

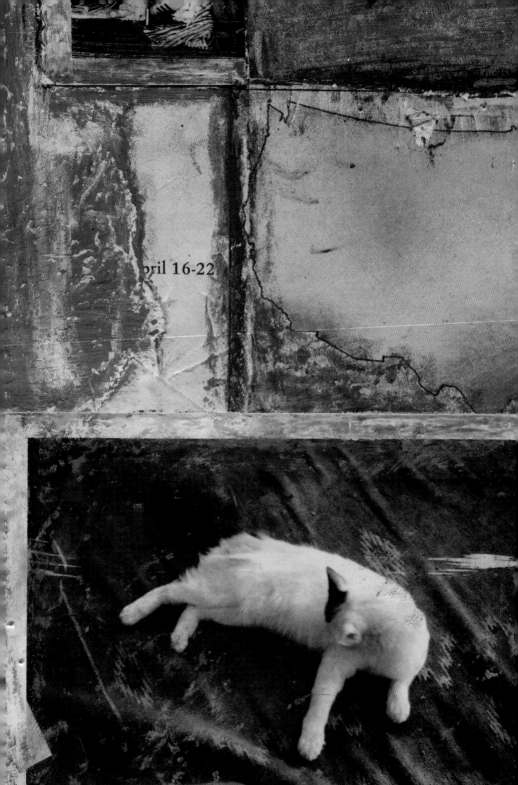

pril 16-22

RADAR ON THE RUG

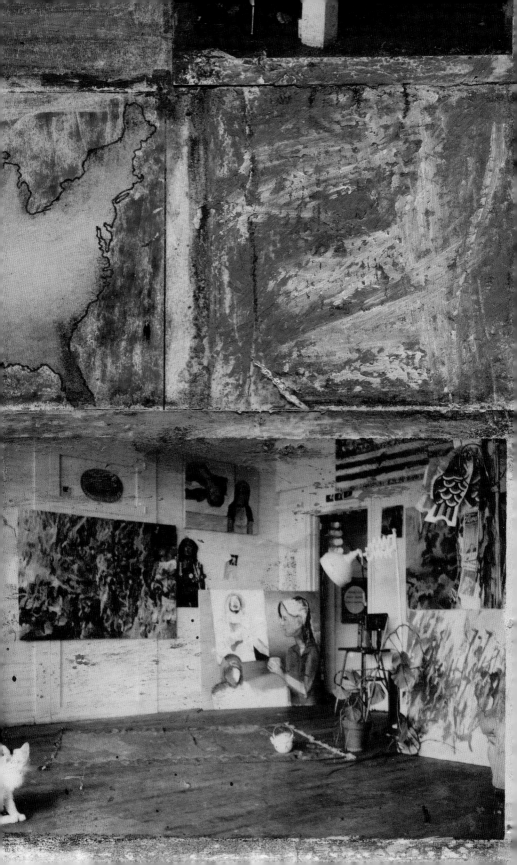

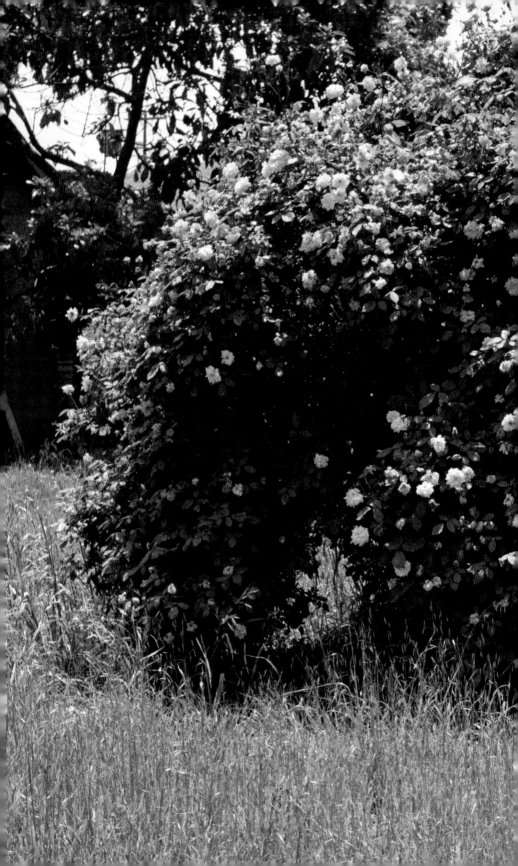

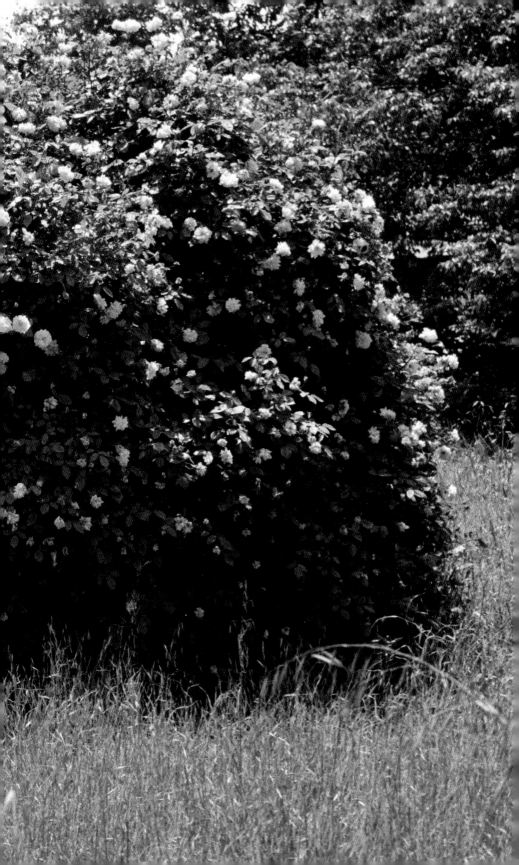

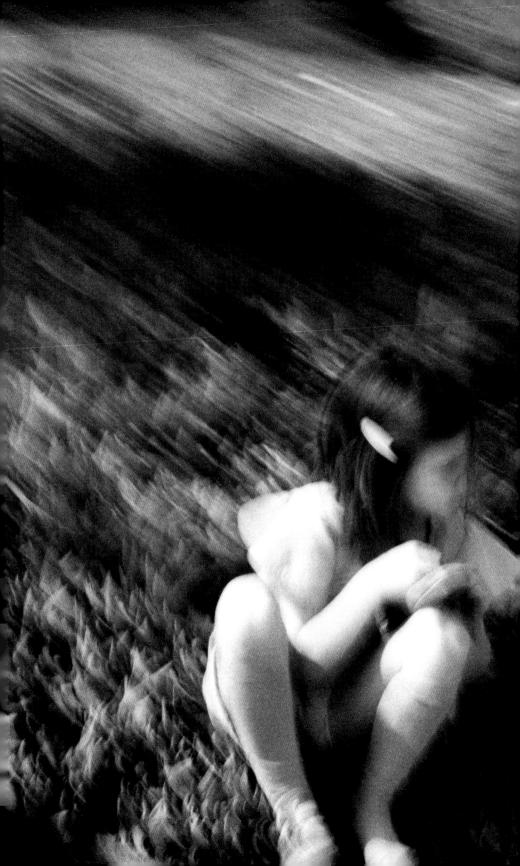

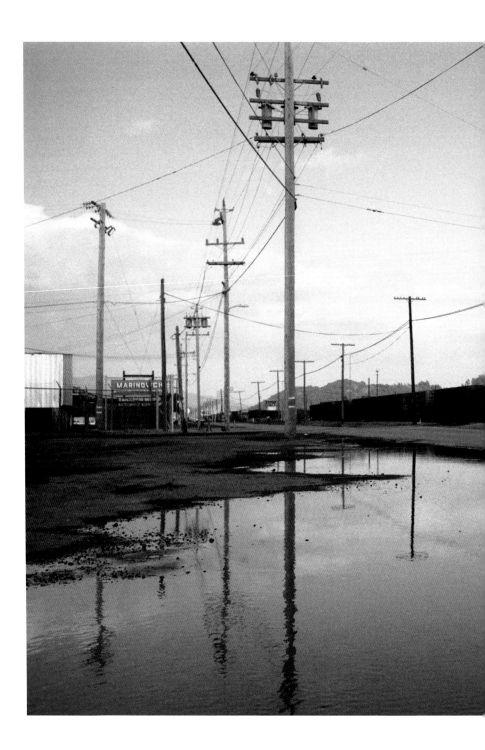

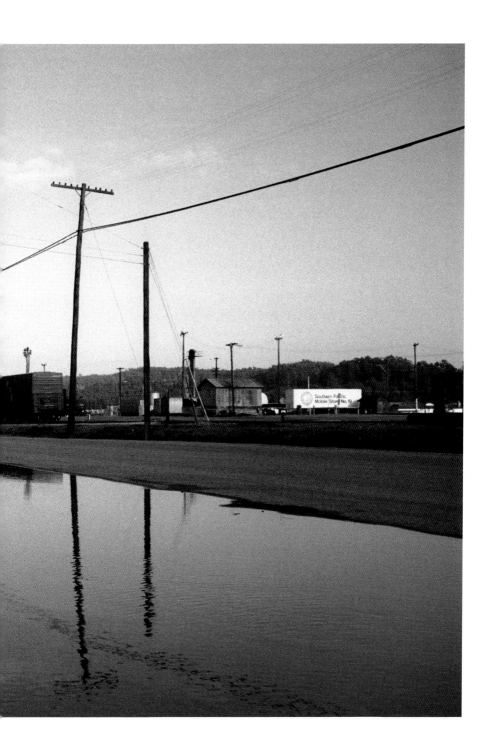

"Addie, why didn't Mom come with us to Mexico?" I asked. At that moment I felt like a real baby even though I was going on thirteen, almost a grownup as far as I was concerned. We'd been squeezed together side-by-side in the cab of the semi for going on ten miles, which took us thirty minutes in the L.A. traffic.

"Well, that's a good question. She would ask, 'Why didn't Dad stay with us in Tomales?' She was really smart, practical. She didn't want to pull up her roots like that and kill what we had there. But she also understood he had to go, that was it, that was the experience he wanted. So she encouraged him and split us apart at the same time. It's sad to look back on it like this."

"I wish you were there in Mexico. I always felt something, like I was on the edge of danger, like the volcanoes were about to blow or something. I learned so much about people. I even learned about Dad. People need to be closer to nature and we don't live that way here. In Redlands we don't get any closer to a real tornado than the Bowl. Tornadoes make cool music, that's all we know. So maybe that's what he was looking for, something more substantial than what happens here in California. I experienced good and bad things with Dad, but in Mexico those seemed to go together all the time. We were closer to what's real, life and death.

"Addie... listen...I...uh...felt...uh...experienced real darkness there, real hatred and violence. It's here too but we are really sheltered. Kids I knew from the neighborhood beat the shit out of this girl, Ramona, the mechanic's daughter. I saw it happen. They wanted something from her...they hated her 'cause she was different. I'll never forget the look in her eyes. The strange thing is, for about a minute I wanted to join their gang. I still hate myself for it, always will. But I also saw the most beautiful things in Mexico. Maybe the bad things helped me notice the good ones more, you think?"

"Kip, all I know is I want to go to the beach. You're thinking too much. Listen, Mom's dead and Dad's not so happy about it. Maybe he wants to blame himself, just like you feel guilty for all the bad shit other people do. I don't even care where I go, I just want to get out of here as fast as possible."

"Look at that, a billion people buzzing around out there, but that's not near as many people as stars in the galaxy," the truck driver injected, like an IV dripping nourishment into a sick patient. He was chewing on a cigar, arching his back, and rubbing his eyes as he looked out on the lights of L.A., which started to fill the horizon as they blinked on with the sunset. "I came all the way across the country and this is what I see coming into the coast.

I never get tired of it. The sun is always setting when I head into La La Land. I plan it that way. I always stop for pancakes in Redlands. I time it so I can see the sun setting over L.A. It's quite a sight. Hey, I thought you two were visiting your uncle."

"What are you, an amateur astronomer?" Addie sensed his sudden concern. "Uncle Danny's going to take us to Malibu Beach—like tomorrow. He lives there with his girlfriend. She's a big actress. I can't wait. She's going to teach us to surf like Gidget. Look out there, that's L.A., Kip, it's 'another world,' just like on that TV soap Dad started watching to numb out. Wow, this view is something, like we're looking down on Earth from a spaceship."

After another hour of stop-and-go on the freeway, we hit the interchange and turned south onto I-5. The trucker slowed to drop us off in Redondo Beach. "I'm heading down to the port so I can't get you any closer than this," he said. "You have change for the phone? Call your uncle and he'll pick you up. The beach is there, down Artesia about a mile, if you want to check it out." He nodded toward the fading light to the west as we hopped down from the cab. The scream of shifting gears and wheels picking up speed dissolved into the hum of waves, barely audible under the din of traffic crawling along the highway.

Addie and I stopped to get our bearings, looking north toward Malibu, south toward the port, east to the mountains, then west at the oversaturated glow of a diner. A sign blinked "Open-24-Hours" in bright script; the red and blue neon stood out like a torch against the graying sky. "Hey, remember when we were kids back in Tomales? And we stole that guy's kayak from town, pushed it out through the mud?" Addie started talking to reassure me that she had everything under control. "We took it all the way out to the end of Tomales Bay, past Dillon Beach to the ocean. And he didn't even know it was gone. We were going to run away from home and make a camp that was just ours. No parents. This is just the same, only we're not playing like little kids anymore. This time's for real." It took a few beats for me to take in what she was saying.

I started to shiver, wrapped my arms around my body, and nodded west toward the neon lights. I hadn't contemplated leaving home until just that moment and I knew I wasn't prepared to do that. But I also knew that Addie was, and her eyes were wide open to the risk and adventure of it. "Let's walk," Addie said, pointing toward the beach. "C'mon, follow the sound of the waves." We crossed over and headed west, slowly at first, then picking up the pace.

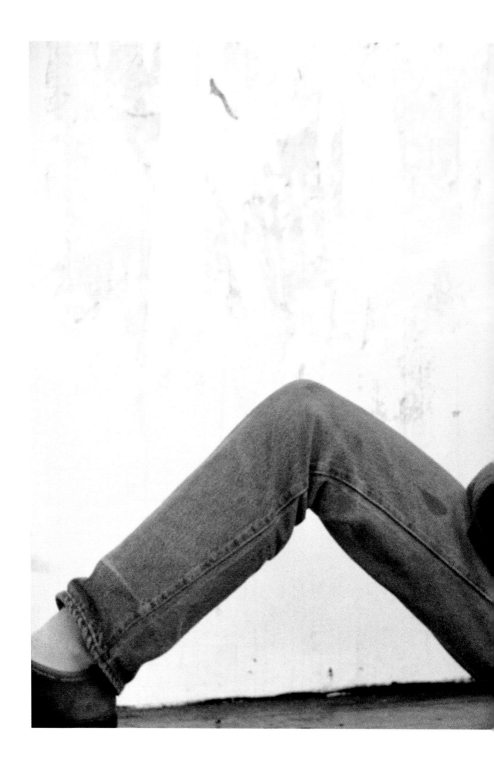

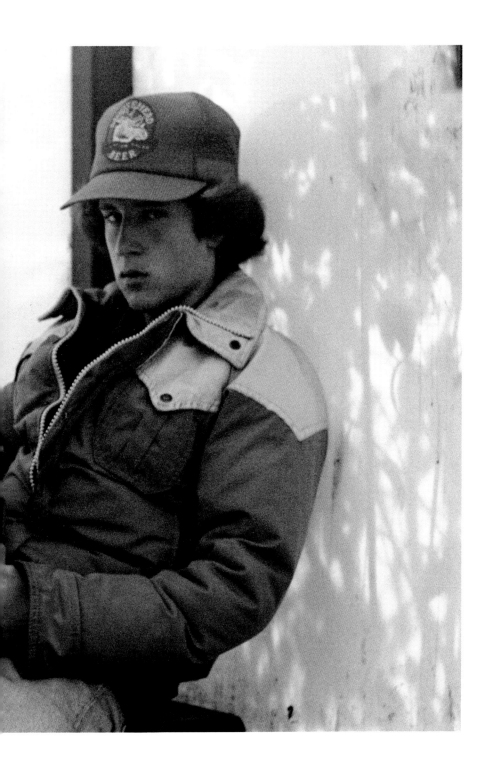

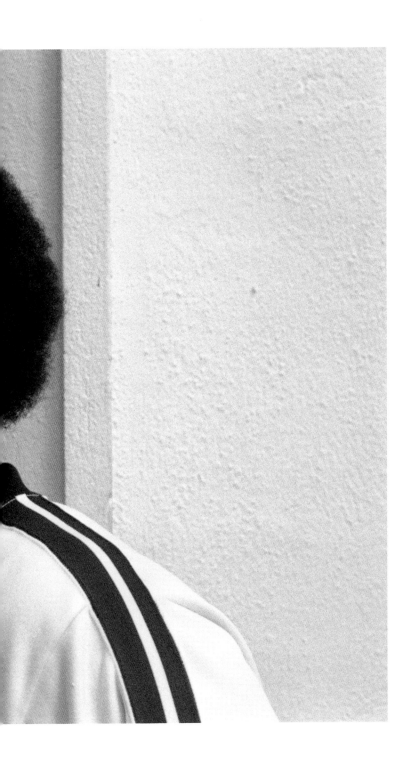

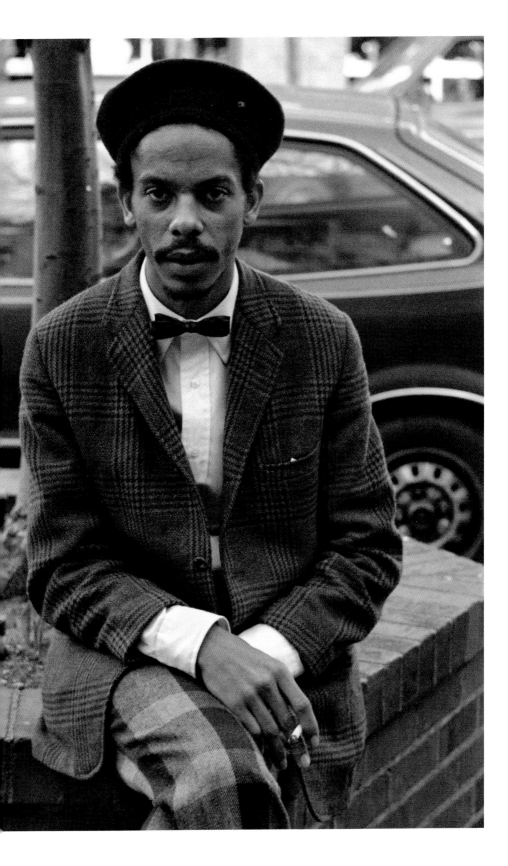

"I'm going back…uh, tomorrow…I have to go back to school at the end of summer," I told Addie. "You do too. Mom really wanted us to graduate; you know that. I'm cold."

A scream echoed back and forth across alley walls. Guitar riffs and syncopated bops imitated Jan and Dean drag city drumming and the smell of cigarettes and incense mixed with something else; all this was injected into the salt air and dissipated, like one of those fourth-period science experiments that never worked. It was both familiar and very odd, unexpected, not at all like the fertilizer-mixed-with-pesticide smell of Redlands.

We bought sandwiches and Pepsi from a deli and kept walking.

"Stay with me, just overnight. We can sleep on the beach…make a fire… tell stories. We can do whatever we fucking want, there's nobody here to say no. Listen Kip, we don't even know each other that good but I feel really connected to you. I guess I'm just barely old enough to have a past, but I do have memories. Do you understand? I wish Mom and Dad could have stayed together longer; then we'd have had more time to hang out. It wouldn't have been so hard for us. I'm really glad you got to visit Mom before she died. She always worried she would never see you again…talked about you all the time like a lost jewel. But listen, I'm the one who stayed with her out in the woods, took care of her when she got sick. At first it seemed like time stopped, like *The Twilight Zone.* But when you watch someone you love get sicker and older, everything just speeds up so fast."

"I miss her too, Addie. Listen, I'll stay with you tonight. Jeez, what are you going to do? What are you looking for out here?"

"Kip, some people think running is like looking for an actual place, like Canaan, or some other desert oasis. It's not like that for me. Canaan was a real place all right but it doesn't exist anymore. That's how I feel about home. It's not there the way you think. It's an imaginary idea from snapshots or home movies and stuff. It's memories. You can't buy 'em and you can't go there. So the place I'm looking for is something I have to create for myself. Wow, maybe I'll go to San Diego…that's very real and I heard the waves are good there." Addie stopped and looked me in the eye. "You go back tomorrow morning, I'll help you get a ride." I was surprised at how smart she was, and I was scared about where she was headed.

"Will you shut the fuck up?" I whispered so no one could hear but me. It was dark now, with few stars. Customized cars were cruising raucously up and down Artesia. A man with a beard approached to sell us something but thought better of it when he realized that I was such a baby compared to most kids on the street. The red and white lights on the wings of planes were flashing very low to the north. The airport was right on the beach and I realized we must be very close.

"Addie, look down there, down the hill." The ocean and sky were one, black on black. The land just ended and fell off into nothing. The flickering lights of about a million campfires spread out across the beach, looking for all the world like falling stars. "Make a wish!"

"I wish I was about twenty-five, sophisticated, smoking Chesterfields at the beach and listening to the Tornadoes on break from my job, which pays a lot but isn't very hard by the way. So I have a lot of spare time for surfin'. How 'bout you?"

I paused for a moment before deciding what to say, looking out for that faint line where the sky and sea come together, and finding nothing there.

"I want to go on a steamer up the Inside Passage. Know where that is? It's in Canada mostly. That's way past L.A., way past Tomales; if you sail up the coast to Canada, then all the way to Alaska, you cross through the Inside Passage. It's sheltered from the ocean by tons of islands. Mom's dad worked there before he died, running ships through the channel like threading a needle. She came here from Canada, did you know that?"

Addie rolled her eyes like she'd heard this stuff about a million times before, then sped up the pace, totally set on reaching the beach.

I stopped to take off my shoes when we finally hit the sand. It still felt a bit warm on my skin, almost balmy, holding heat from the sun like a beach towel wrung out damp and hung up to dry in the evening air. The heat of the sand offset the chill, but I was getting cold. I started to search the beach for driftwood to build a fire. Walking away from Addie, I looked out at the dark ocean and it all seemed so final to me. Looking back at my sister, then away again, I saw that the waves stretched as far as I could see in both directions, close enough to touch but very distant. I watched the blinking lights in the sky and began to count: one one thousand…two one thousand…three one thousand…. Exactly a minute after their rapid ascent over the water, the jets from LAX each started a slow bank south or north, depending on their route; south to Mexico and points east or north up to San Francisco and beyond. Addie came up beside me and then ran ahead, turning to laugh, splashing me with the ice-cold water. Wow, we were playing again like when we were little. I shook it off and ran toward a group of kids around a fire to ask about wood. I had to get warm and I followed the pulse of music.

A girl was singing and a couple others hummed along. Everybody clapped out a serious gospel rhythm at one point in the song. It sounded like my dad's blues records or something I had heard on TV about people protesting in the South. As I got closer I began to hear the words rising up from the sand like sparks from the fire. First a pop, then little specks of light jumped every which way and splintered skyward, dancing orange flashes carving up the night sky like a conductor leading a band in a funky bossa nova beat. The lyrics formed out of the blackness and the rhythm congealed into a tangible song:

> Oh the rock cried out, I can't hide you
> The rock cried out, ain't goin' hide you
> All on that day
> I said, Rock, what's a matter with you, Rock?
> Don't you see I need you, Rock?
> All on dem day
> I run to the river, it was bleedin'
> I run to the sea, it was bleedin'
> I run to the sea...

The song carried and stopped me in my tracks. I wondered about a feeling that could bring the sea to bleed like that, and I realized that this was an image from the imagination, something triggered by despair and a search for salvation.

> Oh sinnerman, where you gonna run to
> Sinnerman, where you gonna run to
> Sinnerman, where you gonna run to
> All on dem day.

Many times on the sidewalks of Mexico City I had watched los indios shouldering a heavy wooden cross, dragging it down the street, a burden they accepted but one that crushed them beyond their physical limits. There were also people hanging in the sky, crucifixes about fifteen feet off the ground, complete with the crown of thorns you see in all those grisly paintings. There were statues of Christ everywhere, bleeding red like in the song. But my memories were a mixed up jumble of images: Ramona's dress covered with mud, masked wrestlers posing on street corners, calaveras dancing and laughing to poke fun at death, and a boy sweeping the street in the first light of sunrise. There was a real mystery to it:

> Sinnerman, oughta be praying
> Yo sinnerman, you oughta be prayin'
> All on that day

This night was different than any I had experienced before. Even the in-cantations of *Día de los Muertos* parades I had followed through alleys around *Catedral Metropolitana* are found in very old traditions that I sort of understood. I had once tried to make a drawing of light reflecting off water and learned I couldn't picture something that I couldn't adequately describe in words. The music I was hearing was like that; it lived inside and outside my head. In this song, the ocean was a living, breathing, bleeding thing that only became real to me as I heard people singing those words. So maybe I could draw a picture of it.

I was shivering...waiting for Addie to catch up. When she did, I felt her arm curl around my shoulders, sharing the warmth two people bring to each other. One guy in the circle caught her eye; he was somewhat older, about eighteen. Looking at me, he motioned for us to join the group. "You cold? Air's got a chill now," he shouted over the song. "Plenty of room by the fire." He smiled when I noticed him looking at Addie. She was enjoying the at-tention and looked away, then back, moving into the circle so her light eyes glowed blood red in the firelight. She was comfortable out here by the water, flirtatious and warming up, but I was looking for a way out. We sat down close to each other as the clapping and singing got more intense. Then the song ended abruptly in a series of whoops, with everyone singing and shouting:

Power...Power...
Power to the Lord.

Even the Wolfman couldn't dish out this stuff on late-night radio, and that's a fact. I swear I had never heard anything like that song and thought it could well be one of the seven wonders of the musical world. I was glad I came to the beach with Addie but now I was ready to go home. The singer was finished and everyone sat down to talk and share some of the dope one kid was passing. Stoking the fire with a stick to watch the sparks shoot skyward, he said he bought it off a stewardess in Manhattan Beach. Addie leaned in to get closer to the fire and rested her head on my shoulder. I wish that moment could have lasted forever but I knew it couldn't. The guy who invited us into the circle was still dancing in a slow, deliberate, circular motion and Addie said to no one in particular, "I'll go back." Then she looked right at me, innocent, like a little girl again. "We've seen the ocean now and I don't want Dad to worry about you. Let's go home."

Addie called Dad, explaining in detail where we were, and now he was coming to get us. He almost lost it on the phone, crying, yelling that he

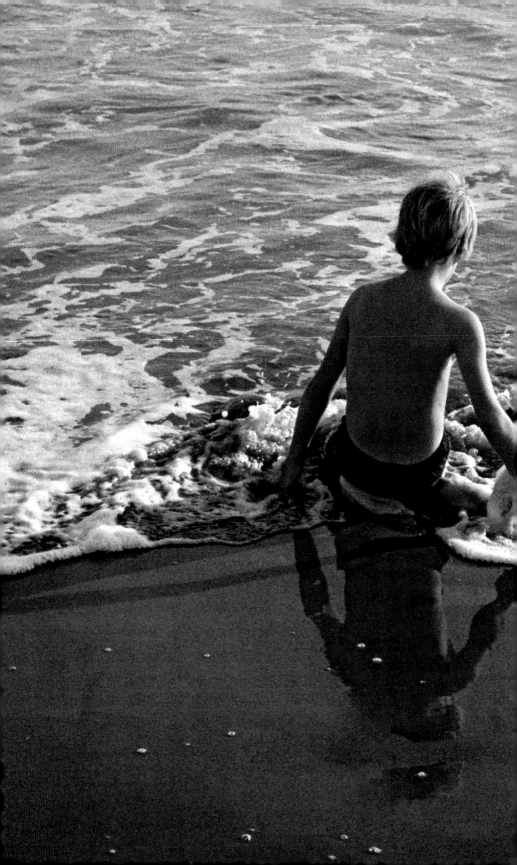

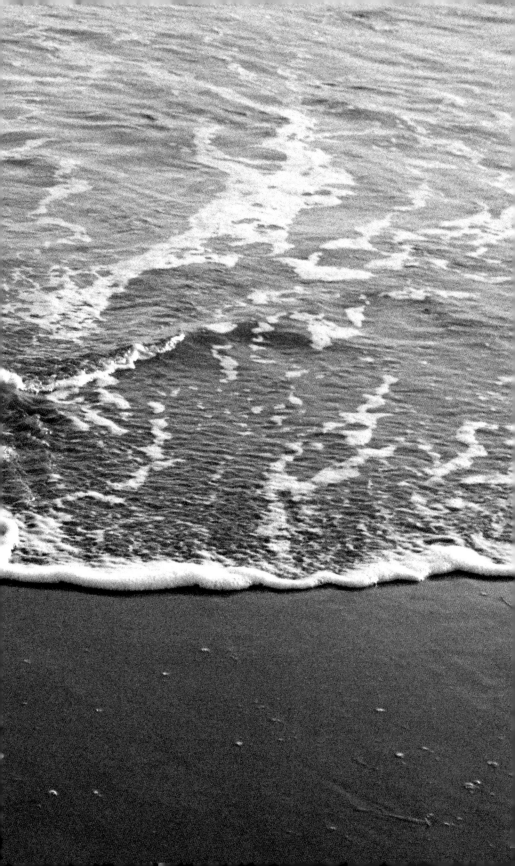

thought we were dead and he'd never see us again. Addie was cool; she apologized and said it was her fault and she would never disappear like that again.

We decided to wait back in the 24-hour diner by the freeway. We only had about five dollars left between us, so we split a cheeseburger and fries, with coffee and a Coke for me. The waitress reminded me of Mom, only a lot younger. She was wearing an apron that looked like it was made from the curtains in our house back in Redlands, and adorned with an unflattering bow that didn't fit the cookie-cutter-modern look of the place. A plastic nametag gave away her name, J-U-D-Y, which was stamped in the same white glossy capital letters I had seen on Mom's filing cabinets at home. Sniffing the air, she seemed serious like she was working the night shift to advance to the next level, which was probably college or getting married. "You kids smell like the beach; smoke from the fire's in your hair."

"Well, Judy, the beach is on fire and the ocean's bleeding, far as I can tell," Addie joked, drumming her hands on the table while she talked so the waitress wouldn't think we were there alone, out late eating cheeseburgers and drinking Coke on the lam (which was true). I smiled and acted polite and very grown up, which made Addie smile.

"So how would you like the burger, raw?" Judy asked, playing along and setting us slightly more at ease. "You could take it back to the beach and cook it on a stick with marshmallows." Maybe she wouldn't turn us in to the cops, I thought. Maybe she was only here after getting kicked out of stewardess school at PSA and she felt sorry for two shivering and scared kids who seemed worse off than she was.

Addie posed the question: "Is five dollars enough? Our dad's coming to get us in a while."

"I'll make it work," Judy said, tightening her lips and calculating around a two-bit tip as the window signs lit up her plain face in masks of alternating blue and red neon. "Water?" She walked off to put in the order before we could answer.

"Listen Addie, you have to tell me what really happened with you and Mom. I don't just want to hear some sad story, tell me the truth. Are you okay? You seem different to me."

"Course I'm different, I'm fifteen now, it's been a long time, Kip. You have no clue what I went through with Mom in the past few years. I guess I'm old enough—grown up now—even though sometimes I feel like I'm still a baby. Listen, Mom had a lot of issues and I took care of her while you and Dad

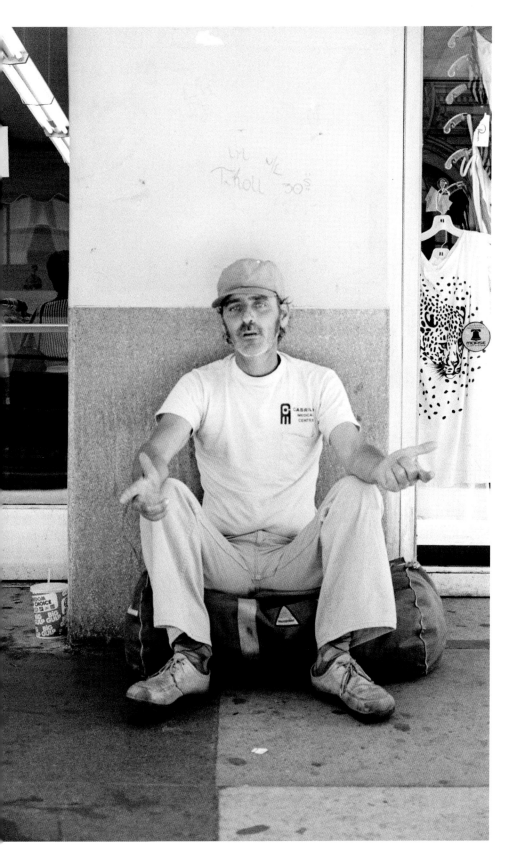

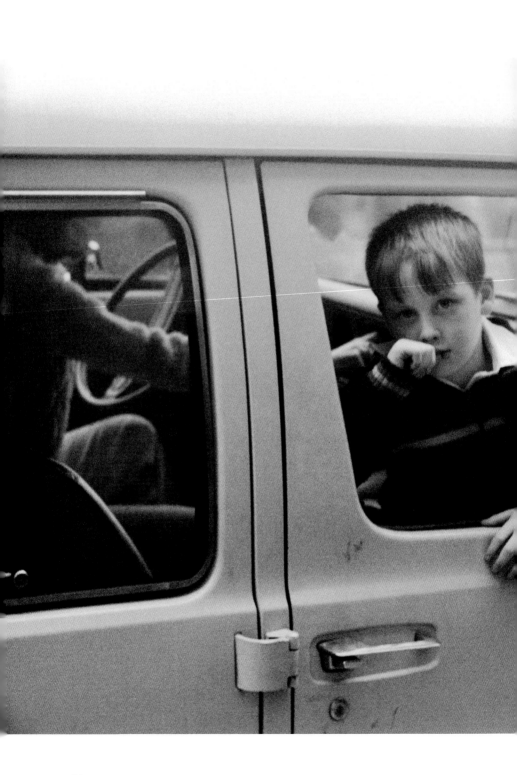

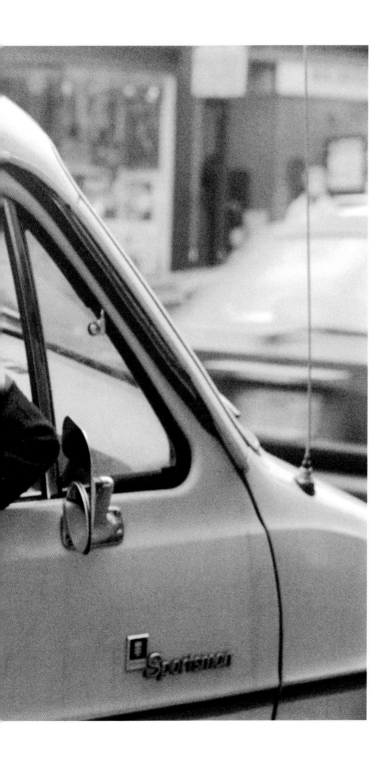

were in Mexico. She never could do what she wanted and then lost all hope when she got sick. I took her to the doctor, cooked, cleaned up after her, did the shopping and watered the garden, read to her…. That's right, I read to her—newspapers, adventure books, *Ladies' Home Journal*—I did this every night for a year. I learned to make Campbell's fucking Soup casseroles from every different kind you could find in Tomales, which is not a lot.

"Mom talked to me about growing up in Nanaimo, babbling on about going north on the steamers with her dad when she was a kid, bringing in supplies to the Haida camps and bringing out beautiful little argillite carvings, like totems. She remembered watching the seagulls follow the fishing boats up the Inside Passage to Ketchikan. The birds saw the fishermen as an easy mark, so they hitched along, sitting on the railings making a real racket begging for handouts. See, the fishermen would toss all their scraps over the side: food, garbage, cut-up fish parts. Everything they didn't need got heaved. After a while, the gulls didn't have to work very hard for a meal; the banquet table was set for them. So they got lazy and dumb, and the eagles started preying on the gulls. They didn't attack the flocks or nothin', just killed them off when they were alone, slowly, one by one. Turns out this really helped the eagles, 'cause the seagulls would eat their eggs. But now all they ate was garbage, which was easier and less dangerous to get."

"Weird."

"Mom said it's 'survival of the smartest,' just like with people, like any mob of Madison Avenue businessmen on a Sunday afternoon, hanging out at the club with friends, smoking cigarettes and looking for a handout. Somebody starts to count on the easy deal…that makes 'em lazy…and they stop paying attention to the stuff they really need to remember to do their business. Soon enough, someone bigger and meaner comes along and takes away everything. To me it means we have to pay attention to the essentials, stay smart, and not get lazy and carried away all the time. You know, stick to the music."

The waitress brought two glasses of ice water, and Addie immediately grabbed the Heinz 57 off the table and poured it into her glass, stirring ketchup into the water so it turned an eerie blood red. "It's a trick I learned from guys on the street in San Francisco."

I looked her in the eye. "What guys?"

"I used to go into the city to get away…couldn't stay home with Mom all the time. I felt locked up in prison like I'd done something wrong, which I

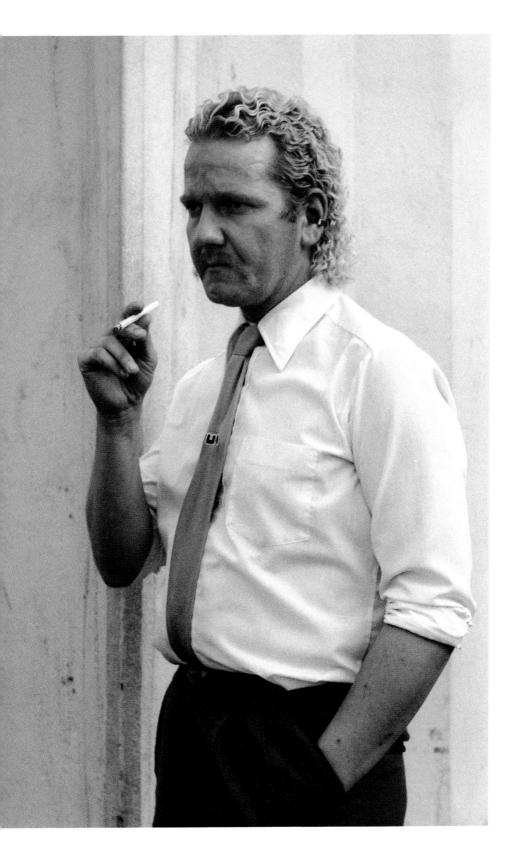

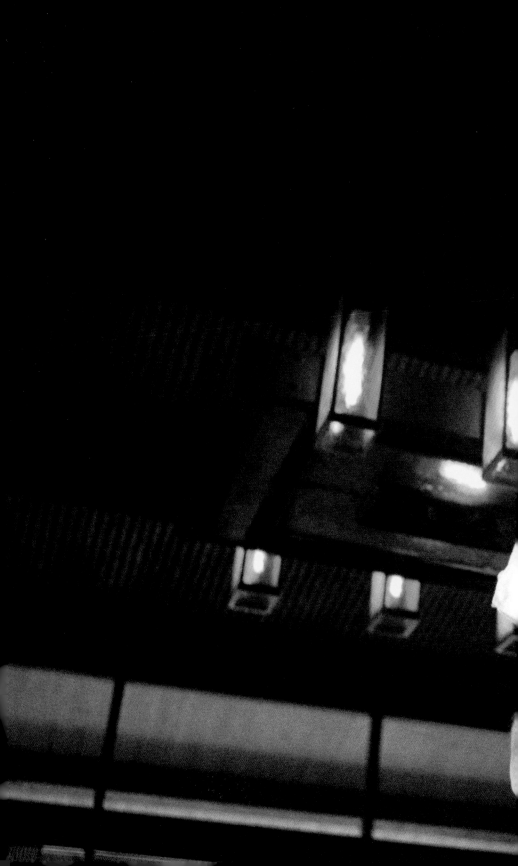

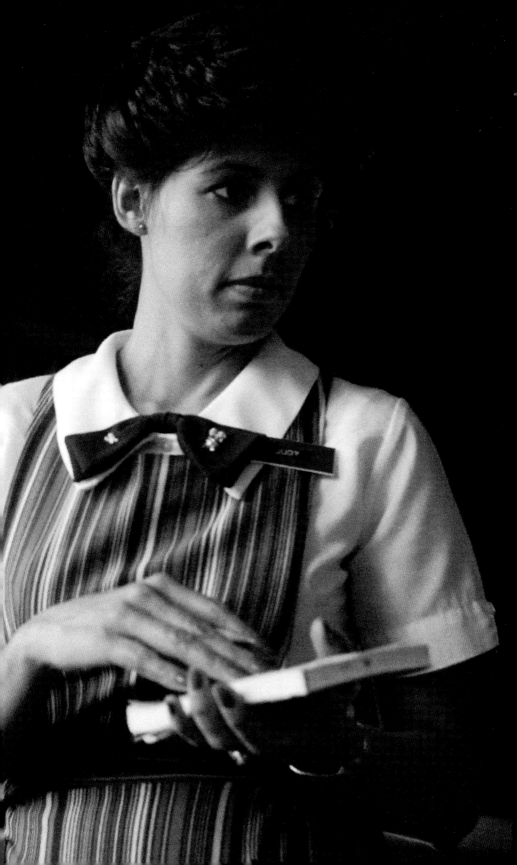

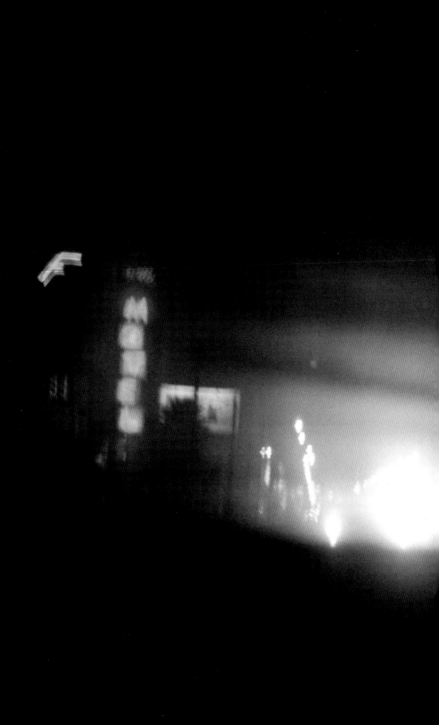

hadn't. I would take the bus from Point Reyes Station," she shrugged. "I stayed away sometimes, just for a few days, the most was maybe a week. It drove Mom crazy. Listen, if you're on the street and you're really hungry you can go into a coffee shop, order something, and ask for water." She looked again at the ketchup bottle and nodded. "It keeps your gut from hurting too bad for about an hour. Plus you can add sugar which is good for you, gives you energy." She held up the glass, which looked even redder in the neon glow of the diner. "Then you leave as quietly as possible—when no one's looking—before they bring your order." She sipped the concoction and scrunched her face, adjusting to the taste, then, holding her nose, gulped it down and used a spoon to get the last bit of ketchup from the bottom of the glass. She wet her lips with her tongue and stared at the table.

"I don't know what to do, Kip. I thought I'd feel more...uh, more free now that Tomales is behind us, but I don't. Guess I just need to accept what's happening. That's what Dad says, anyway."

The waitress came by a few minutes later and set down the burger between us. She studied the empty glass, spied the last of the ketchup at the bottom, smiled, and picked it up. "More water?"

"Sure," Addie said. "You want mustard with your burger?" She looked right at me and pushed the plate across the table. "That's for you, little brother. You must be hungry."

"Come on, share with me," I begged. Addie shook her head. "Why did Mom...uh, I mean...why did she do that to us? I mean...why did she have to die? She seemed fine before we left for Mexico. She helped me get ready to leave. I was sad but she really cheered me up. I didn't see anything different in her face. She actually seemed happy for the first time in awhile."

Addie doused the fries in ketchup and started picking at them. She was hungry too, so I pushed the plate back into the middle of the table. She looked serious, like Mom did when she was about to cry. "I don't think she meant to hurt you, Kip. I know she didn't. She didn't have a choice, damn it." Her voice rose in pitch and she started sniffling. "Mom seemed to get really old really fast, it was scary. Her body gave out but her mind...it was like she was a kid again, sharp as a knife, and her memories were like little razors cutting into her, painful and gratifying at the same time. She couldn't remember her own mother except from photographs. She was too young when her mother died and that really hurt her. She told me she was torn when she met Dad, because she thought if she went with him she'd never have a chance to do what she wanted. Getting married meant staying home with kids. She could never become the person she dreamed about...a famous scientist...save the world...and all that crap. She gave up her dream for us and struggled with that her whole life. That split what she wanted and what she did, it never added up for her. But at the same time, what she did was probably the only thing she could do then. She was an orphan. That's how it works, you can't go back and do it over."

"Let me...ask...you this," I said with my mouth full of burger, chewing on my words, trying to pretend I wasn't upset. I was afraid Dad would arrive and then she'd clam up. "Do you think she blamed us for her problems? I mean...Mom never seemed comfortable in Tomales with all the stinking oysters and hippies. She never seemed quite at home with two kids and a cat. Remember when she'd take us with her into the city or that trip to L.A.? And she'd drag us around buying nice clothes and going to museums. It's like she was on a mission to connect with the world—with history—the same as with the research she did when she was younger. She had to make that connection to the past.

"I remember how she used to show me picture books of famous paintings and she always went back to one, the *Agony in the Garden* by Mantegna, or something like that. Jesus is there in a blue robe, kneeling on this funky rock, and he's praying with a bunch of very serious little naked babies, only they're angels, standing there on a cloud looking down at him. He's checking them out like he could reach right out and touch them, they are that solid. It's like a dream and they're showing him how he's going to die. It's so sad, I wonder why she loved that painting so much."

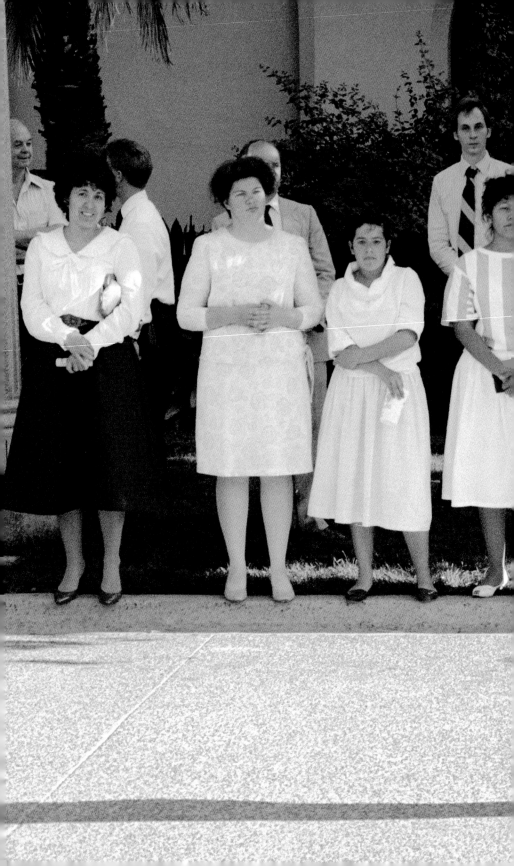

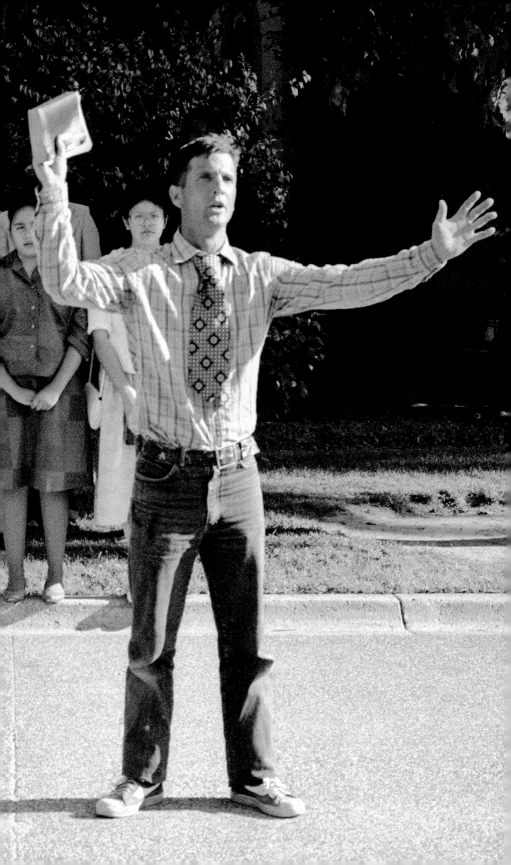

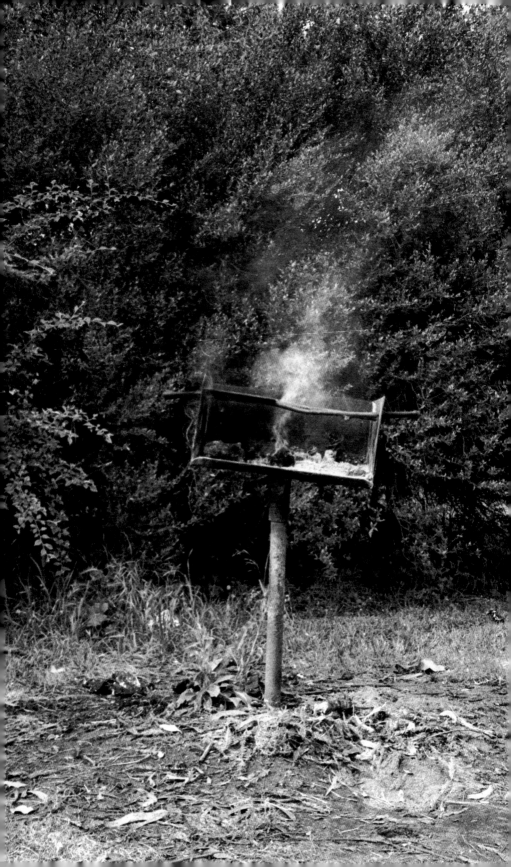

Santa Cruz, California, 1975

There's an arcade that runs though an alley between streets in downtown Santa Cruz. It's small, not at all like those grand arcades you see in big cities, and the walls are covered with murals depicting Aztec gods and the pyramids of Tenochtitlán. I dreamed that I walked in from Front Street by the poker place, went right through, and when I came out the other side I was in New York City. There I was on the street—I think it was Delancey or Canal—way downtown, cars and trucks everywhere. And when I got there I found a poem written on a scrap of paper and kept it for later. I didn't read it.

Santa Cruz is really small and funky compared to New York, which is why I came here from Redlands a year ago. Man, you think the surf scene took over Redlands in the sixties? Santa Cruz had it too but magnified a million times, plus we have real waves here. I thought I could get work as a logger or maybe a tour guide, but that didn't happen. Even though you still see trucks hauling trees out of the mountains, people are making stuff here now. Manufacturing. And agriculture. The money's better. To get a job in the fields you gotta join the farmworker's union. So instead I went to work at the cannery and then at a place that makes little colored plastic boxes. It's all piecework. You get paid for washing and cutting up tons of broccoli or beans or strawberries. And if you don't finish you don't get paid. You have to work super fast and your feet start to hurt after a few hours...then your back... then your mind goes numb. Sometimes I talked to this girl on the line and she hated it too. "The work is shit and your brain goes mushy in about an hour. It hurts my hands; stays that way all day," she told me. "After six or seven hours everything hurts—every muscle in my body—'cause you keep doing the same thing over and over. You never get used to it. The fog comes in late and hangs around till noon. It soaks into everything. My shirt gets damp and cold and I can't breathe. But the worst thing, you know, that shit is covered in chemicals. It gets in your lungs and you start coughing. I've been here off and on over a year."

"How old are you?" I asked. I was twenty-three and pretty much on my own. I thought she looked about twenty.

"Eighteen...ah...seventeen and a bit more. Listen...don't stay here too long. That's my advice. And don't tell anyone how old I am. Understand? My advice, get another job. My aunt worked Watsonville for seventeen years, raised three kids during that time, and she had to quit at thirty-seven 'cause her hands hurt so bad she couldn't go on. I want to go to L.A. and model."

"What's your name?"

"Uh, break's over. I'll see you again."

After my shift I punched out and left the shed, mostly thinking about the short walk back to Beach Flats, where I lived. I saw the girl again, standing at the edge of the gravel lot smoking a Camel and staring off into a row of tall Eucalyptus trees—a windbreak planted years ago by the railroad—that shot a piercing smell across the field. A few trucks were starting to come in with brussels sprouts for the late line. The sun was down already and the fog sat over the bay with real malice, like a bad guy trying to ease into town after dark without being noticed.

"Can I get a smoke?" I yelled across the lot before approaching her from behind. She turned her head with a look of surprise, making sure I totally understood she didn't really smoke before offering up her last one. "Kip," I said, putting out my hand like any other acquaintance from the line. "Well, I never got your name so I wanted to introduce myself." She turned back stoically to watch the fog advance against the darkening sky.

After the sun went down, the temperature dropped about ten degrees in ten minutes. "The beach is just over there past those trees. Hear it?" She looked up and her face was illuminated for a few seconds by the lights of another truck entering the lot, this one filled with green beans from Watsonville. The smoke from her Camel filled the hi-beam and danced in the light, then disappeared in blackness as the truck backed up to the dock. I noticed how young she was and thought about leaving for home as she turned and caught my arm. "Angie…Angie Correa," she offered.

I quit my job at the cannery after about two months. Angie was right, everything hurt at the end of the day plus it was totally a dead end, a fast track to oblivion. The plastic box factory wasn't much better. It took the same amount of skill (none) and was just as bad for my morale (hopeless), but the work was less repetitive so I stuck at it long enough to save up for the summer and no more. I calculated that about $1,500 should last me four months and I'd better have it all figured out by September or it's back to the factory life. The boxes were actually interesting to look at, modern and clean, used as packaging for fancy cosmetics. We made thousands every day in translucent red, orange, yellow, green, blue, purple; you could line them up and make a rainbow. Machines did all the work and we ran the machines. At least it wasn't all piecework on a line like the cannery.

Angie and I still saw each other sometimes, mostly at a bar by the harbor where we liked to sit outside after work and watch the fishing boats come in and out of the fog. She told me she was born in L.A. but her parents had come into California from Mexico in the late fifties. She was the baby in her family, the only one who was born here and didn't need papers to stay. Throughout the fifties, her parents travelled back and forth across the border at Nogales, working as *braceros* on farms in Arizona or sometimes traveling across the Mojave in pickups, "to work the Coachella Valley or on to L.A. doing packing or sewing for better pay. With three kids to support, it got too hard for them to live the migrant life," she told me one night, sitting outside under colored Christmas lights that stayed up all year round. "So they moved north up the coast, first to San Juan Bautista and then Watsonville."

"San Juan Bautista? Wasn't he the one that Che threw out of Cuba for being such a corrupt asshole?" I was trying to make her laugh. She smelled like strawberries, which were ripening in the fields and were being processed every day down at the cannery.

"You never understand anything," she shot back. "Juan Bautista was a Spanish conquistador who came north from Mexico to colonize Alta California. This used to be a Spanish colony like Mexico and San Juan was a pawn, not a saint. He led a mission to convert the Indians or kill them. We learned all that in school, you know."

"Why did they call you Angie? Your mom and dad, why did they call you that? Where's the name come from?"

"My friends call me Angie. My parents call me Angelica, like an angel with wings, you know. I guess after two other crazy girls they needed someone to help them talk to God and I was it," she answered, closing one eye and pretending to peer through a spyglass, on high alert for ghost ships entering the harbor through the fog.

"That's a tall order," I said.

"Well, sometimes I wish I really got the wings that were supposed to come with the job. That would make communicating a lot easier, don't you think? Sometimes I dream that I'm flying." She eased in and out of a pensive state; one minute she was giggling about angels or the latest episode of *All in the Family* (a show her mom just loved) and the next she was spitting into the wind about colonialism. I liked how she could easily imagine things that didn't exist and bring them to life. I signaled the waitress for an order of the homemade enchiladas we liked to split.

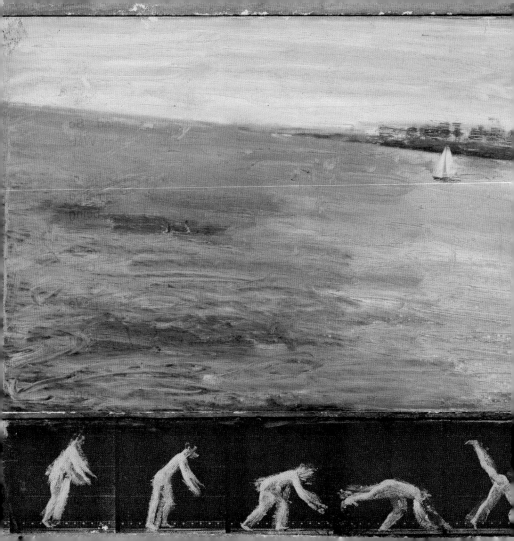

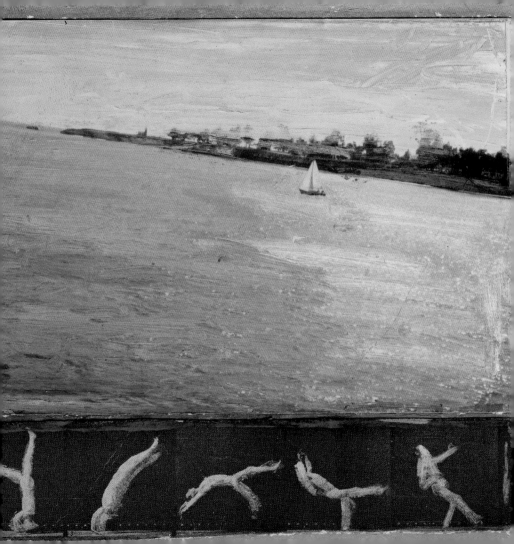

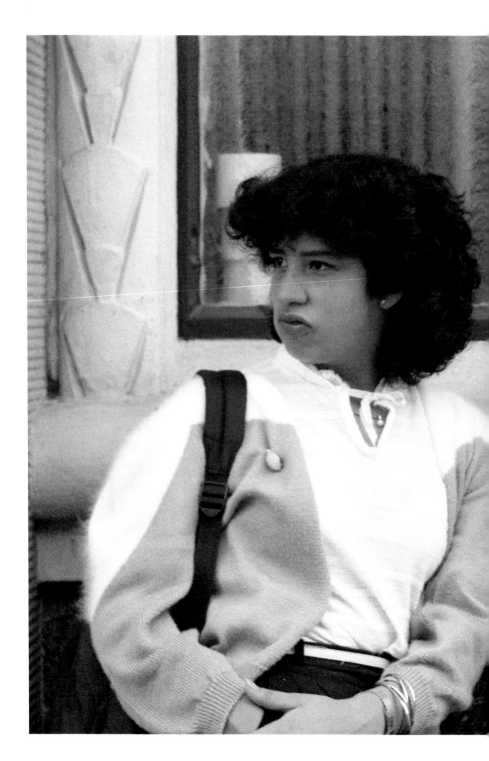

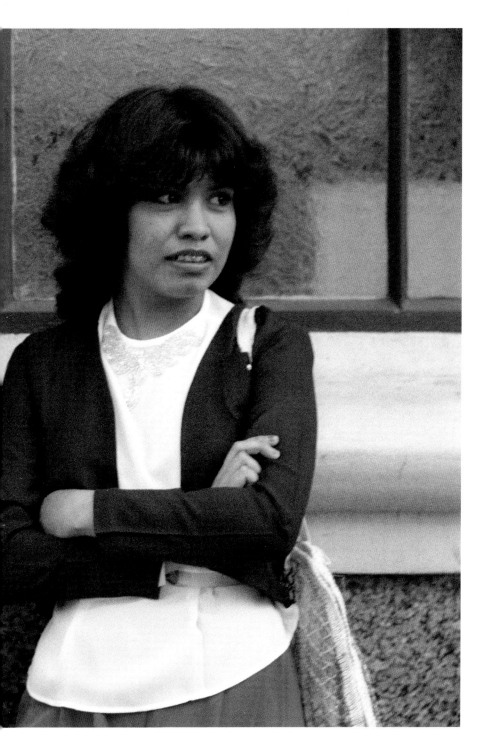

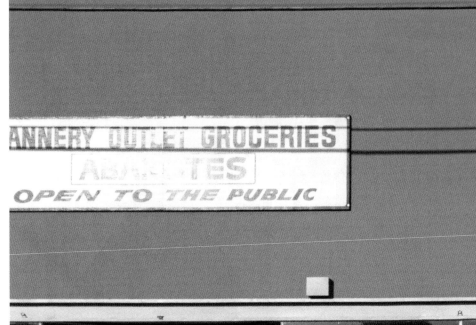

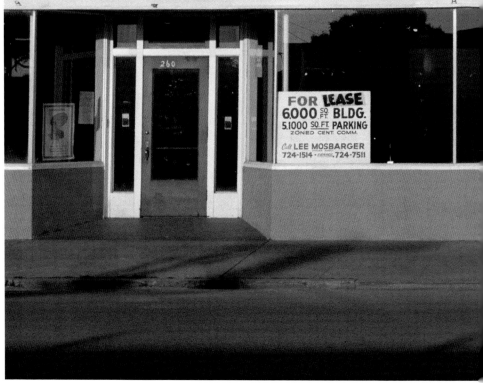

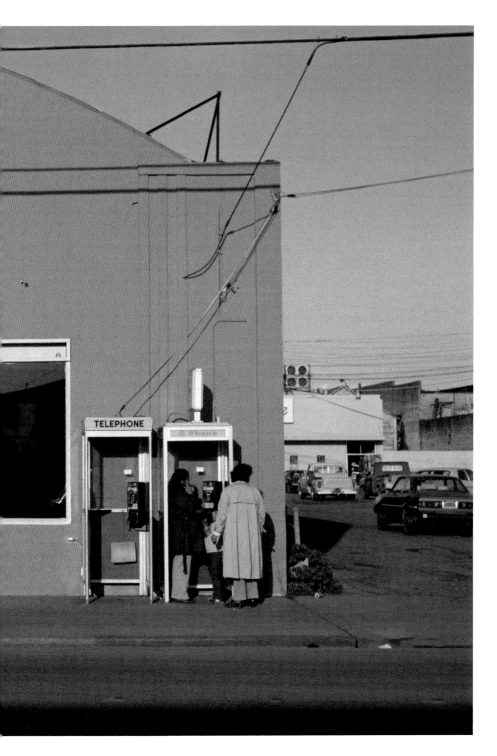

"Everyone dreams they're flying. Ever write poetry?" I asked on a whim.

"Nah, that's for people who have time to think about stuff and study their words. You want my story? Every spring I have to drop out of school to help earn money for my family, doing anything that pays. I used to do laundry, babysitting, worked the fields, anything. My family has connections at the cannery so I've been there two seasons now. You want to hear some poetry? I'll tell you a real story."

I looked at Angie and then up at the sky. There was a sprinkling of stars visible over mountains to the east since the fog bank had stopped short at the coast on its nightly expedition inland. "Listen, my ancestors were Indian people in Mexico. In their stories the universe was created from the body of a sea creature. It seems very mysterious today but this is how we made sense of the world before Colón—Columbus—before the cross became a burden on my people. There were many gods. The first was called Ometecuhtli Omecihuatl—androgynous—a man and woman together just came into being from nothing, like the void, which is hard to imagine unless you're a physicist. This god represented everything that was used to create the universe: male and female, good and bad, heaven and earth, everything. Ometecuhtli Omecihuatl had four children and they represented the four directions. Their names were Xipe Totec in the north, Huizilopochtli in the south, Quetzalcoatl in the east, and Tezcatlipoca in the west. Those dudes are the big four of the Aztec pantheon and between them, they created water and threw in a giant crocodile monster just for fun. Cipactli was really huge and really mean and started eating up everything the gods created. To the gods, this meant war and they cut up Cipactli into different parts, which were used to make heaven, earth, hell, and everything else like stars and stuff. It took a long time because they had to make five different worlds, which they saw as five suns. Known as the jaguar, the wind, the rain, the water, and the earthquake—in that order—these suns were created and destroyed by the gods over and over to populate the world we know today. Even after all that, the monster refused to support life on her back unless she was 'soaked with blood and fed with human hearts'." Angie wiggled two fingers on each hand to make quotation marks in the air, emphasizing the insanity of it all. "The gods agreed and the fifth sun—the earthquake— is the time we live in now. It's supposed to end in a giant earthquake. I mean, wow."

The enchiladas arrived smelling like Calle Carranza, and I remembered how Dad took me to visit the Museo Nacional de Antropología to learn about Aztec culture. Addie was visiting from Tomales, and we ran through the place for hours, completely transported by all this stuff from the past. Tezcatlipoca was god of the night—the smoking mirror cut from polished obsidian—who guided the dualities of war and beauty, time and space. How different was he from the saints who guided the Spanish north on the *camino real* to subdue the indigenous cultures? I looked at the eastern horizon to see if I could tell what time it was from the constellations, and I imagined a universe completely remade in an earthquake that would bring about another time. The landscape was crumbled and graceful bridges spanned giant chasms that rent the ground. Hands on the clocks were rearranged. Like *Planet of the Apes*, there wasn't much left that I recognized.

Angie had to leave before nine to catch the bus home to Watsonville, so we paid the waitress and started walking up Seabright to Soquel, where the last south-bound bus passed by at nine thirty sharp. Holding hands, we walked in total silence.

At the end of the summer I started taking pictures for a company that made postcards. The guy who ran it said there was a big market in town for any snaps of surfers, redwoods, the Mystery Spot, the Last Supper, and the Giant Dipper, a fifty-year-old wooden roller coaster, which for many people is the only reason Santa Cruz even exists. When everything was quiet at the cannery (almost never) you'd sometimes hear people screaming as the lead car went over the top and dropped about a hundred feet straight down in seconds. The wind carried the sound south over the mouth of the San Lorenzo, a pretty sketchy spot under the railroad bridge that was populated by homeless winos and drifters looking for a spot to crash. When conditions were right and the Dipper was cranking, it was the main soundtrack for all the workers living in the Flats.

If you went out on the street late at night after the Boardwalk shut down and everyone went home, there was an eerie quiet. Most people who lived in the tiny bungalows on Park Place worked all day at stand-up jobs and were sleeping then. The repetitive motion of the tides and waves was the only thing that lulled me to sleep. When I lay in bed at night with the light on, trying to put myself to sleep reading pulp fiction, I breathed in the residue of other people's lives, of those who lived here before, the shift workers in the profitable fields of the California coast who had dozed off dreaming of an easier life, if not for themselves, then for their children.

They didn't pay me for the postcard pictures but instead gave me the camera to keep and some extra film—they even developed it for me and

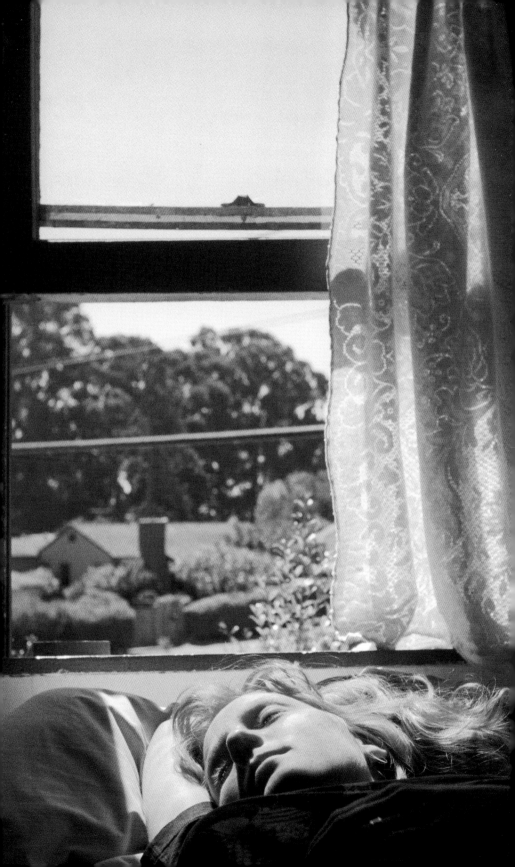

gave me proofs—so I was able to learn some new things about photography and sell a few pictures to the local paper. It's all observer-in-the-street type stuff. Angie encouraged me and was glad I didn't ask her to pose without her clothes on. I had forgotten how much I liked to look at things close up, watching people and making up stories about them. Maybe I'd have a better future if I got back into photography and tried to make it into a real job. I saw a lot of people out selling religion on the corner, so why shouldn't I stand out there and make pictures of it all? I was really thinking about this 'cause my summer money was almost gone.

But instead I got a new job working downtown in the stockroom at Woolworth's. This came with more security (money) and less fun (time to do what I wanted), but I had plans. Angie and I were spending more time together and I wanted to settle down a bit, so when she turned eighteen I invited her to move in with me. She might as well have been moving to Singapore but arrived a few days later with just two things: a toothbrush and her sewing machine. "What's that for?" I asked her abruptly, half expecting her to say she'd been sewing her own clothes since she was three.

Instead she told me, "It's all I have that's worth anything. Maybe I could sell it to help pay the rent." We lay down together late at night, telling stories and listening to people screaming in the streets after the bars closed.

Angie told me her family was totally assimilated into American culture but identified themselves as bicultural, with one foot firmly planted in Mexico and the other in California. I was amazed when she said her older cousin— a farmworker *vato* in Visalia—was deported all the way to Hermosillo before her aunt even knew what was up. She was horrified when I told her about Addie and how I didn't even know where she was. I shared a box of old postcards that Mom had sent to me when I was in Mexico; pictures from nowhere—old highways, rest stops, parks, motels, and diners—she had bought at flea markets just for fun. "This is the real America, the one we don't see anymore," she wrote on the back a card depicting the Golden Spike restaurant next to a Best Western in Promontory, Utah. "This is the place where the railroads came together. Wow. I'm working on a new thesis about bacterial infections in chimpanzees. So don't forget to wash your hands."

On breaks from the stockroom I'd get a Coke from the counter and sit by the big picture window watching all the people go by. There were businessmen, retired government workers, skateboarders, preachers, drifters, students, the postman, lovers, the man who sells show tickets at the Catalyst,

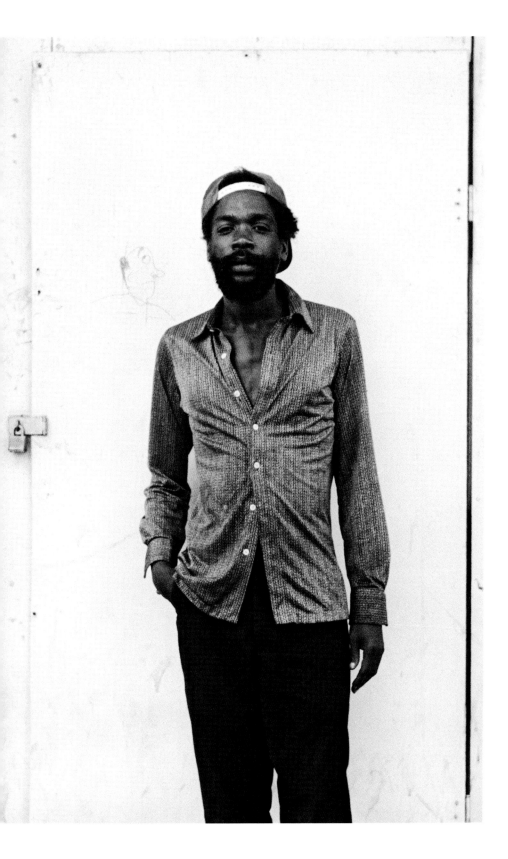

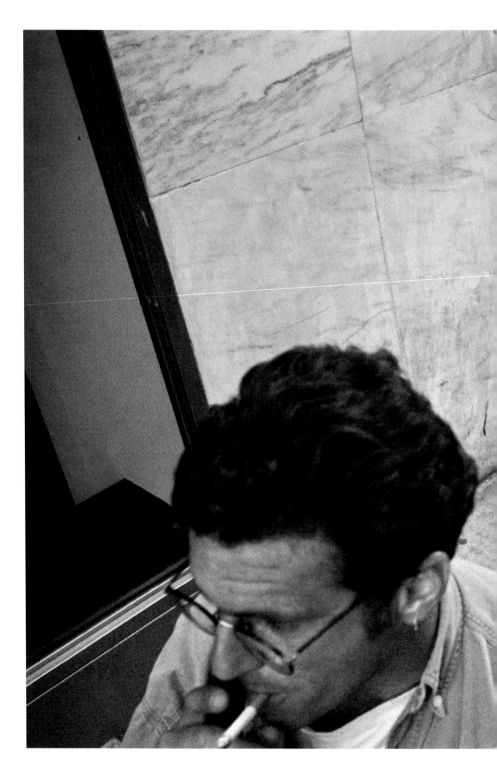

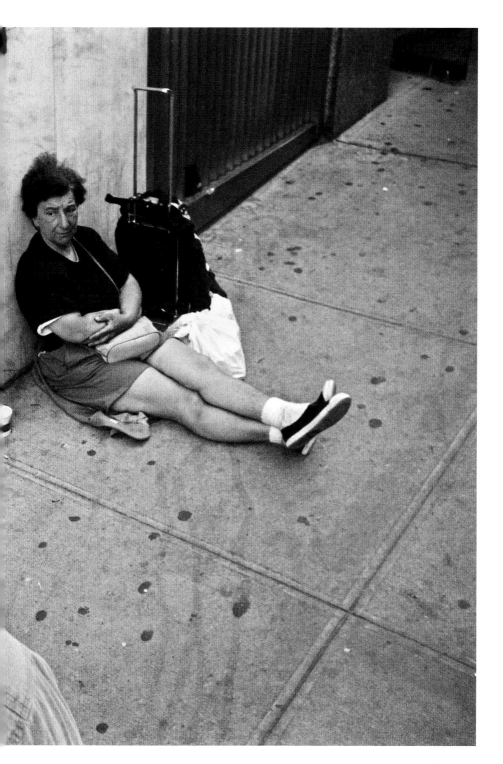

and some fashionable kids from the High Street neighborhood who all wanted to move to L.A. and be lawyers for pop stars. It was like a theater where the play was whatever happened to be going on at the time.

One day I was putting bottles of aspirin out on the shelves and met a guy who was traveling all over the U.S.—the Deep South, Detroit, St. Louis, Arkansas, the Dakotas, Arizona, Albuquerque, Indian reservations, California, everywhere. He said he had a headache, came from Sweden, and was here for a year to make pictures of the real America. He said no one understands what it's really like here, and it was his job to show it like it is. He photographed the saddest things you can imagine: dire poverty, sick people, drugs, crime, institutions, hospitals, lost dogs, murders, roadkill, car crashes, shit overflowing from bad plumbing, everything and anything bad that caught his eye. I actually thought his pictures were pretty good when he showed me what he was doing, and I told him so. I asked him why he made images like that, so sad and real. He said he was just showing what's there, like a witness or a testament. I asked him why he didn't photograph anything beautiful, like landscapes, clouds, hummingbirds, cute girls, protestors, or the reflection of the sky in a puddle after a spring rain. He said he didn't need those things and they weren't true anyway. I asked him how he got money to travel. He said he never worried about money. People always gave it to him when he needed more. I asked what he thought of California. He said the beauty didn't fool him. So I told him to visit Redlands and spend some time with the fruit pickers, and then stop by the rail yards after sunset to blow the seeds off dandelions and watch them float away in the desert wind. He wrote that down in his notebook.

I'd had enough of postcard pictures, and I already knew everybody around the neighborhood from the time I spent watching random people walk by the window at Woolworth's, so I started looking at things that were more abstract—sun, sky, water, and wind—trying to associate nature with words or dreams I had. One afternoon I was out with my camera, walking up the Main Street hill by 2nd, looking back at the pier. I spotted Angie walking down 2nd headed toward the Flats. With the full expanse of Monterey Bay spread out behind her like a wide-screen long shot that introduces a close-up of the heroine, she waved from across Main and shouted at me against the wind. "Kip, you know that stuff you told me the other night, what your sister said about your mother? It can't be right."

She ran right into the street and stopped short as a car whooshed by, then skipped the rest of the way and buried her face in my jacket to warm

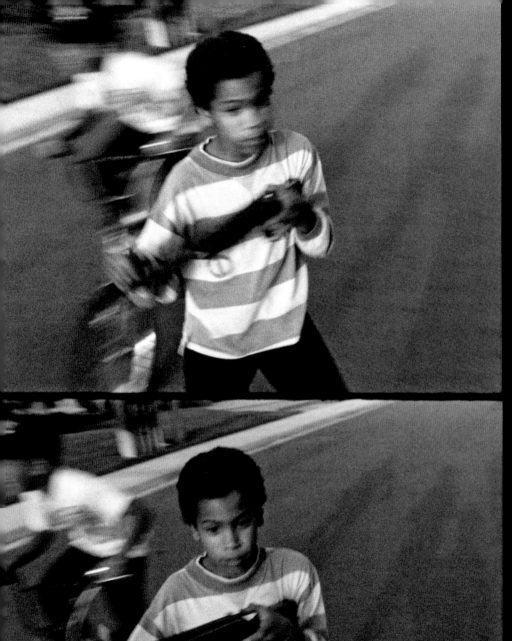
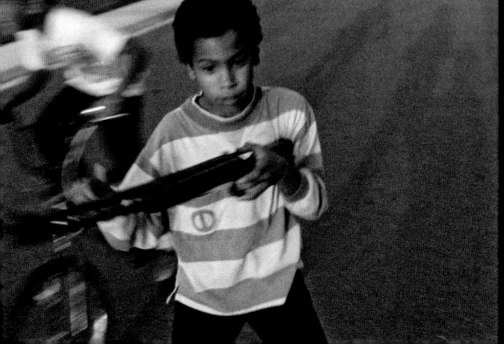

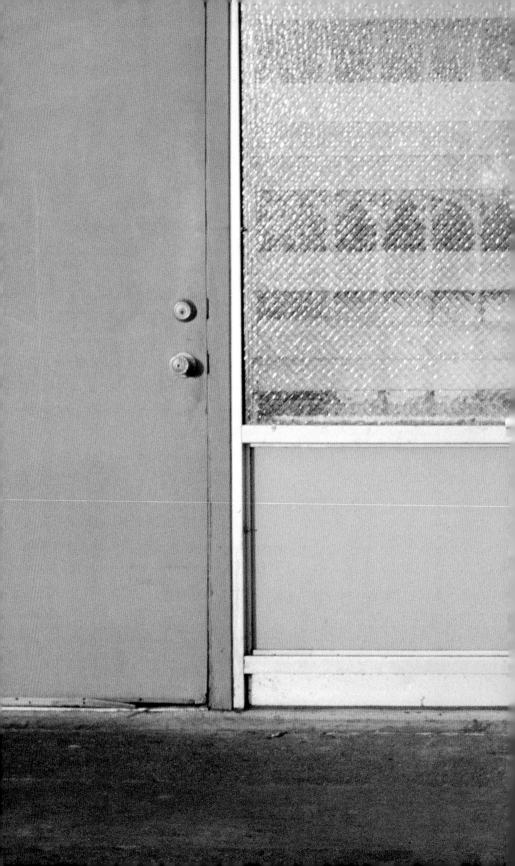

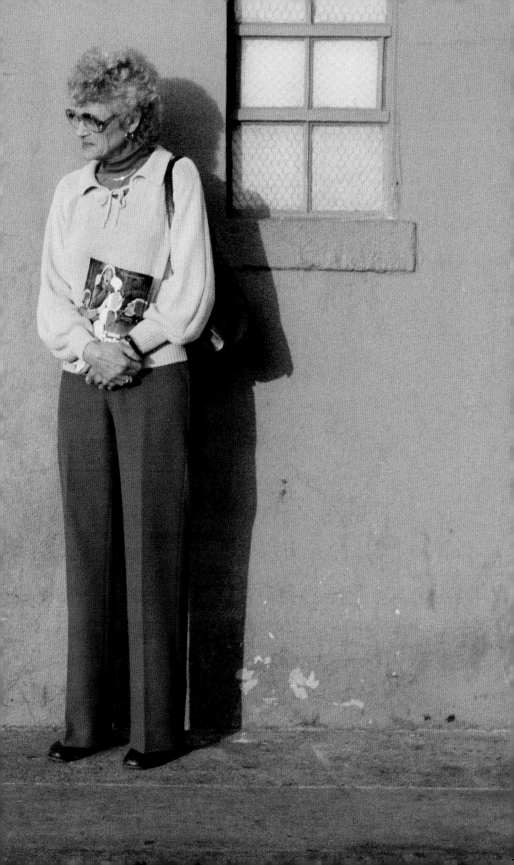

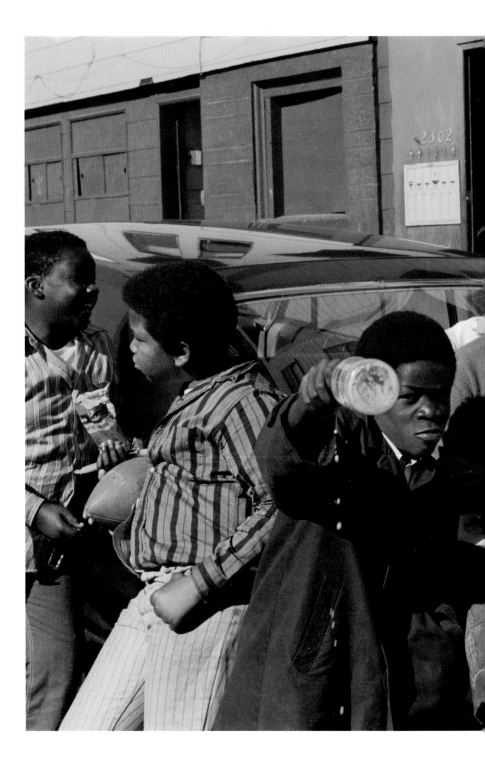

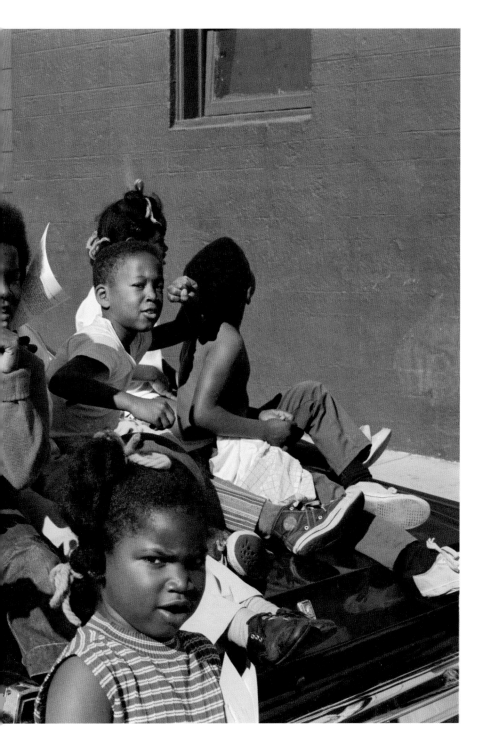

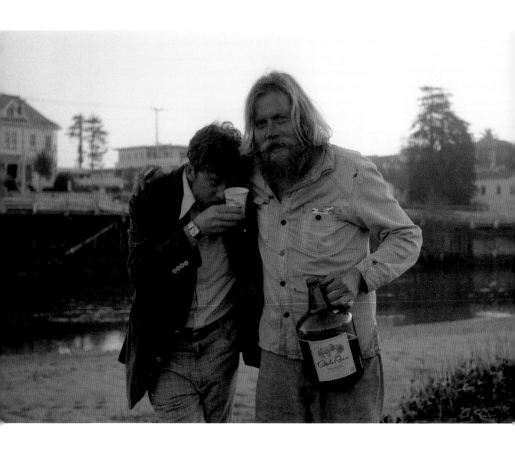

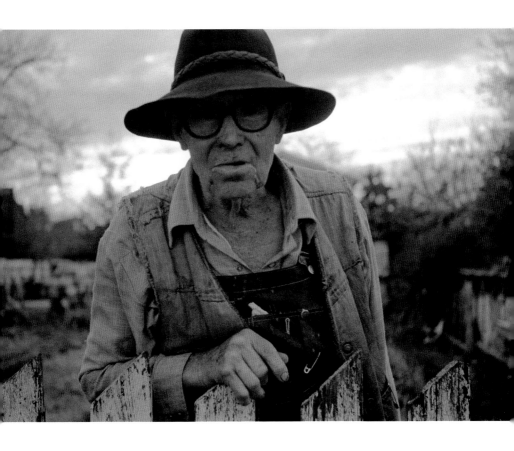

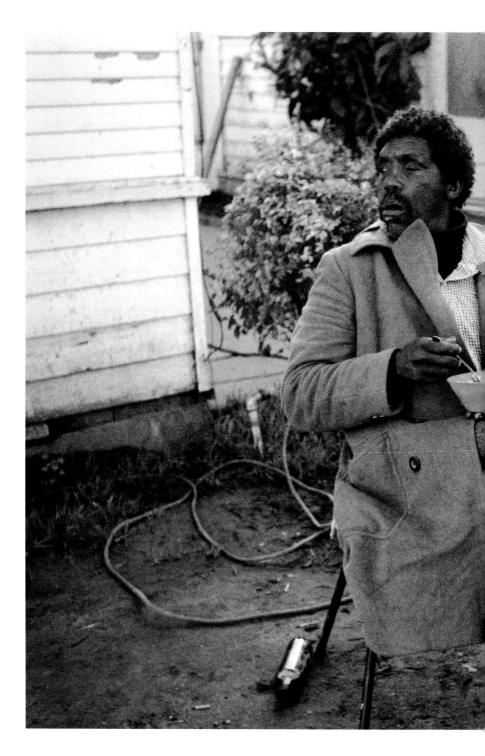

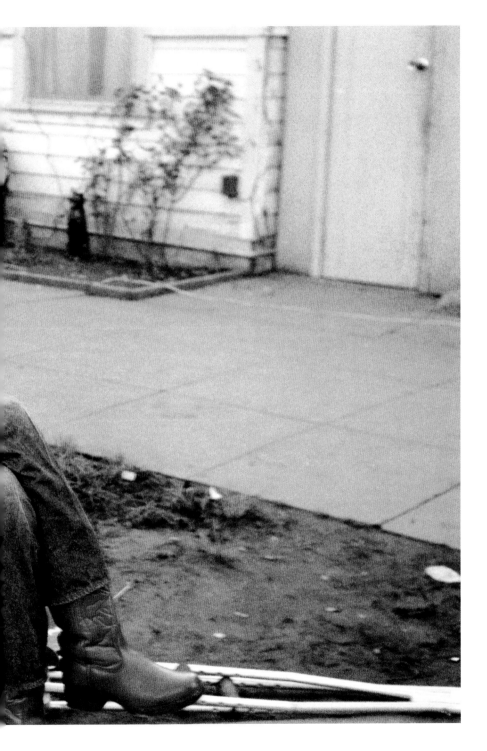

her nose. I felt dizzy and pushed her shoulders back, holding them at arm's length to look her in the eye. "What do you mean, it can't be right?"

"I thought about what you said, that your mother quit her dream job to stay home and then died of cancer." Angie looked across the translucent bay to the PG&E stacks at Moss Landing pumping smoke into the air. Watching it drift away and dissipate as it gained altitude, she turned back with a look I hadn't seen before. "It doesn't make sense to me. I mean, what do you even know about your mother's life during her last ten years? Not much. You were in Mexico. You were in Redlands. You were with your dad the whole time. Why did they even split up? Do you know? I read the postcards you showed me, the ones your mom wrote when you were in Mexico. All she talks about is the past—her work and history and stuff—but she never says anything about how she feels. She never says that she loves you. And she never says anything about Addie."

"What are you, a girl detective in some crime novel? Come on, I don't know. I don't know why they couldn't live together anymore. They didn't love each other, what do you think?" A few cars passed and we could hear the chains of the Giant Dipper straining as they dragged the coaster cars over the top, followed by adrenaline screams that accompanied our descent to Park Place.

"Kip, did you ever question Addie or think your sister wasn't telling you the truth about something...that she's lying to you or holding something back? Hear me out. Your mother was a little bit nuts. You can tell from her writing. I mean who uses that kind of language to write their kids? Your sister is also nuts if you don't already know. She told you she was taking care of your Mom out there in hippie-land. Well, she wasn't. She was living on her own in the city part-time, addicted or something. And your mother was onto her and couldn't do anything about it. As far as I can tell, Jess never even told your dad that Addie was missing."

"How do you know?"

"Addie called last night when you were out with your camera." Angie looked at my old Minolta as if was an instrument from Mars sent to suck the memories out of Earthling brains. "We talked a long time, and I guess she wanted to get this all out in the open. I don't know why she told me this stuff. Maybe it's her way of asking you for help. Listen, Kip, when she was on the street in San Francisco she was really messed up, shooting real shit with no money to back her up. It's a miracle she survived. I mean, how do you think she did it? She was abused by a lot of people. It seems you're the only one in the world she really trusts, and when you left Redlands she split for L.A. and got lost on the street again. Addie never did get along with your dad. He loved you and left you alone but ignored her, and when he did pay attention he was messed up and telling war stories. Those memories haunted him, Kip. He never told his stories to anyone else, just Addie. She said it was like ghosts would appear and take him away. I've got a bad feeling about it. Something bad happened there, something she doesn't want to talk about. I don't know why she told me all this stuff."

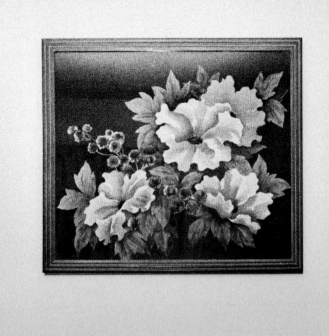
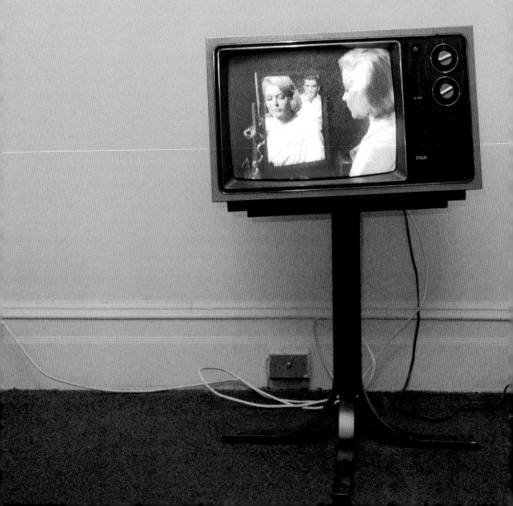

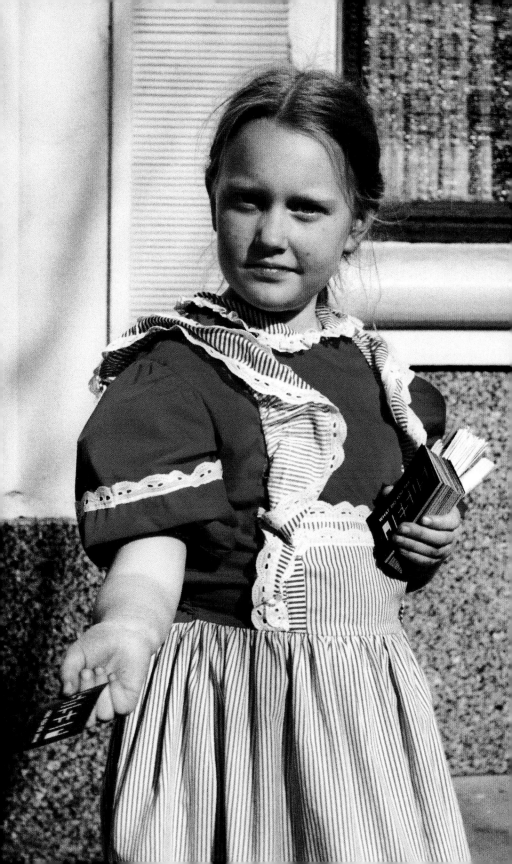

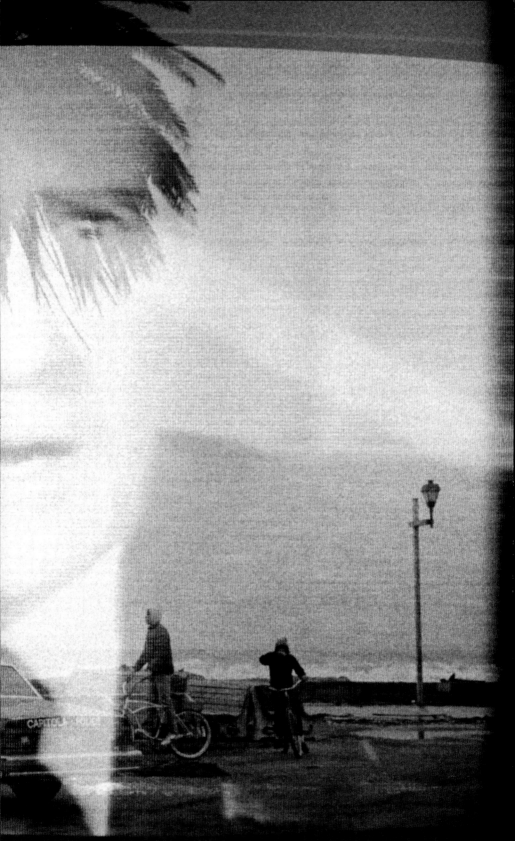

Watsonville, California, 1977

Angie's older sister, Tina (a nickname she got from her uncle, whose favorite singer was Tina Turner), got caught up in a raid on a chicken processing plant in Beaumont, right off the highway, not too far east of Redlands. "They deport almost a million people a year now, they're not kidding around any more," Angie vented into the receiver when her mom called. "I mean, who are they looking for, Al Capone? We have to do something." She calmed down a bit when she learned that her dad was already on his way to pick up Tina in Riverside, where she was let go after her new boyfriend arrived with her green card. It seems *la migra* came in and took everybody who looked even a little bit Mexican, assuming that most people were working there without papers.

I went with Angie to visit her mom, who we found pacing back and forth in the backyard of their small and incredibly neat home off a dirt road by the Pajaro River. A small statue of the Virgin of Guadalupe was stationed next to a bush by the front door, in an arrangement that also featured a garden gnome and a wheelbarrow of potting soil. In the entry I noticed a small altar displaying a mishmash of family snapshots, *Día de los Muertos* sugar skulls, plastic action figures of *Lucha Libre* wrestlers, and pictures of movie stars from the forties and fifties. I recognized some of them—Dolores del Río, Lupe Vélez, Anthony Quinn, and Ricardo Montalbán—from posters in the lobby of the cinema we frequented in Mexico City. Adriana Correa brought us sweet tea with sliced lemons she grew in the yard. She was a compact woman who switched easily between English and Spanish, had the boundless energy to care for her entire family, and focused for the moment on her youngest daughter, who had arrived in a near panic. Just being home calmed Angie enough so she could sit in the yard and carry on a normal conversation. "Angelica, *mira*, Tina's okay, you don't have to worry about her any more. First of all, she can take care of herself. Also, she's legal so they don't have any right to arrest her like that. She's just trying to feed *los hijos, por amor de Dios*. Papa's on the way if she needs help. He'll be there in a few hours."

Angie was still worried, as if this had happened before. "I just hope he gets there before they throw her on the bus to TJ."

Angie introduced me as her friend from the cannery, and Mrs. Correa rolled her eyes, looked me over two or three times (maybe more) and said in that same straightforward manner of her daughter, "Well, you must be pretty strong to stay there more than a few months. That place beats you down and cuts you up into little pieces. I've been arguing with my daughter about it for a while. Angelica, you should be back in school, you know that."

We all laughed when I offered up to Angie's mom that I had already moved on from the cannery to a job in the stockroom at the Santa Cruz Woolworth's. "I think of it as a lateral move. But I'm really a dilletante, you know, a part-time photographer working on my craft. I already sold a few pictures to the paper." I was trying to sound smart, like I had some kind of future, some dream beyond the line at the cannery. I looked up to watch a cloud move across the bright sky, wondering what it would be like to just make beautiful pictures like some of the famous artists whose work I had admired in museums.

After a few minutes of silence, Angie moved into the kitchen to help her mom, who was washing pinto beans in the sink, starting in on dinner for the three of us. I followed her inside and noticed Mrs. Correa's hands—a farm-worker's hands, tough and weathered—expertly cleaning every bean. She saw me watching and signaled me over. "Angelica said you lived in Mexico when you were little. So you know how important it is to wash the beans before cooking them, right? I raised three daughters moving back and forth across the border, following the sun for work. It didn't matter what side of the line we were on, as long as we had beans and rice to feed our kids. You know, these fingers must have touched every single bean the girls ate at home for all those years; it's something special, raising kids like that. You have to provide everything for them until they can do it for themselves. I've thought about it a lot and I have to say, when you touch every bean your family eats, it seems like such a long process but it's not really. They're grown now and that's like a blessing, it gives you a real appreciation of the earth and how hard she works to sustain us."

After dinner we all sat together in the yard waiting for Mr. Correa to call as the Santa Cruz Mountains turned dark green, then purple in the eastern twilight. When the phone rang, Angie jumped up and ran into the house. I could hear her quizzing her father, asking over and over if Tina was home with her kids and what was happening. "Shit, how can they do that? It's not even legal. How much did it cost? Shit."

Mrs. Correa sat still, her arms folded against her chest as protection from the chill. She shook her head, obviously worried about Tina and her grand-children, but also embarrassed by her youngest daughter's temper. "She's like her father, Kip. She assumes everything is straight and right until it isn't.

Then she has a temper like an earthquake. That gets her in trouble." She eased out of her chair and went in the house to confiscate the phone from Angie. When she returned a few minutes later she looked tired for the first time, shaking her head. "You know, when Angelica was kicking me, about to be born, it was still possible to go between states without all these problems." It looked to me like she was addressing the *nopales* growing by the fence, but I knew she was talking to me in confidence. "I had a hunch and dragged myself north to L.A.—I was tired and it wasn't easy—so at least one of my children would be born in this country. Then she would have more control over her own future."

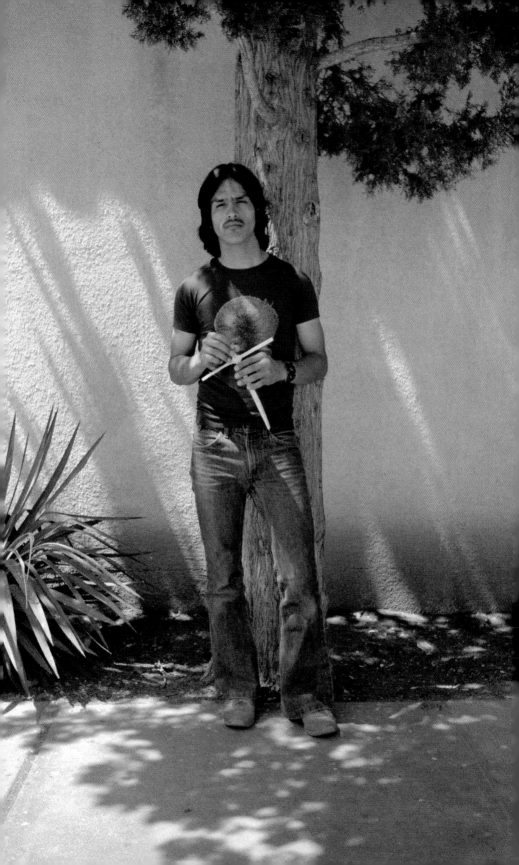

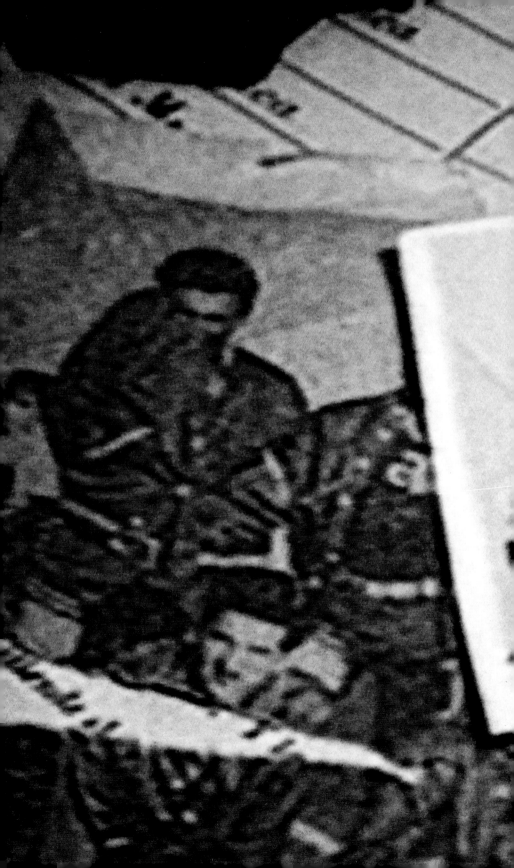

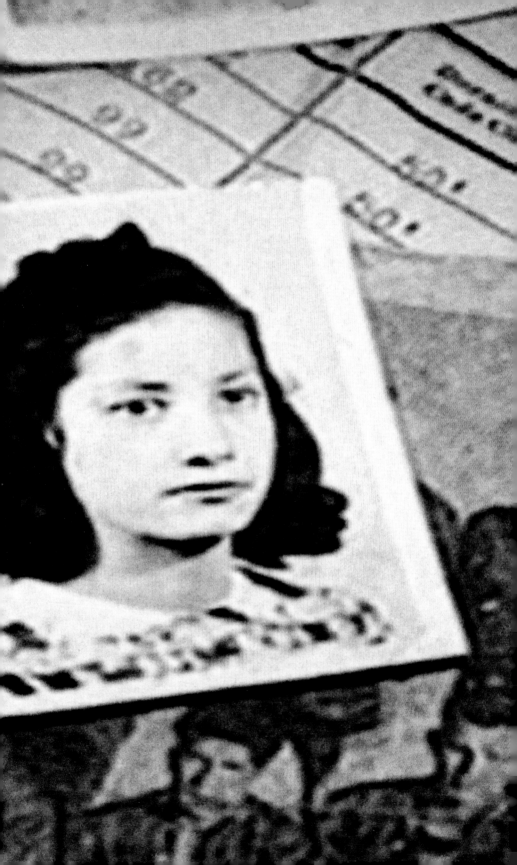

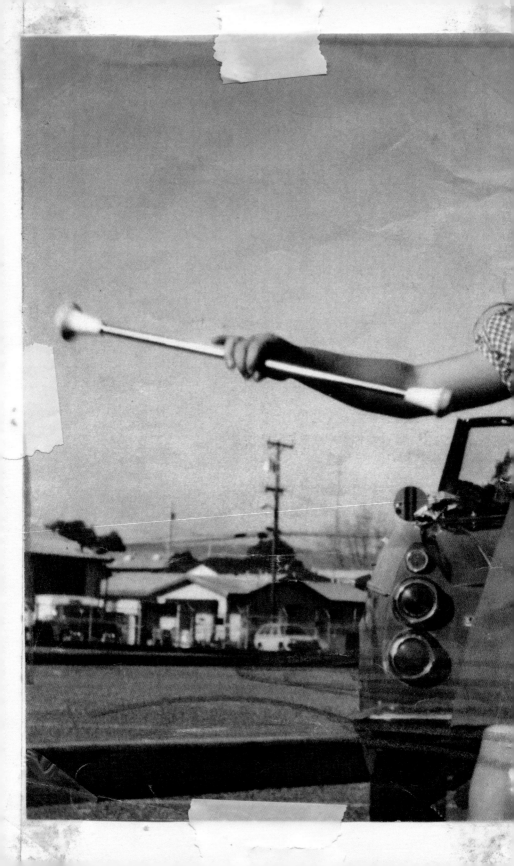

-8

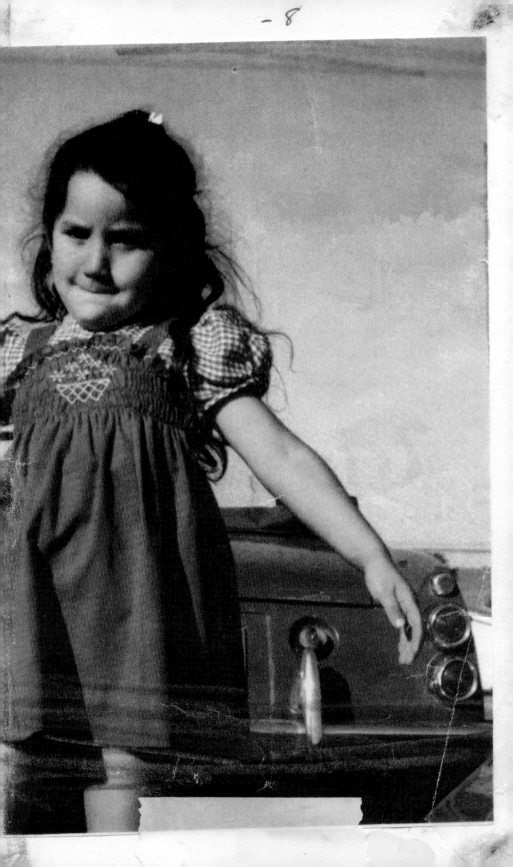

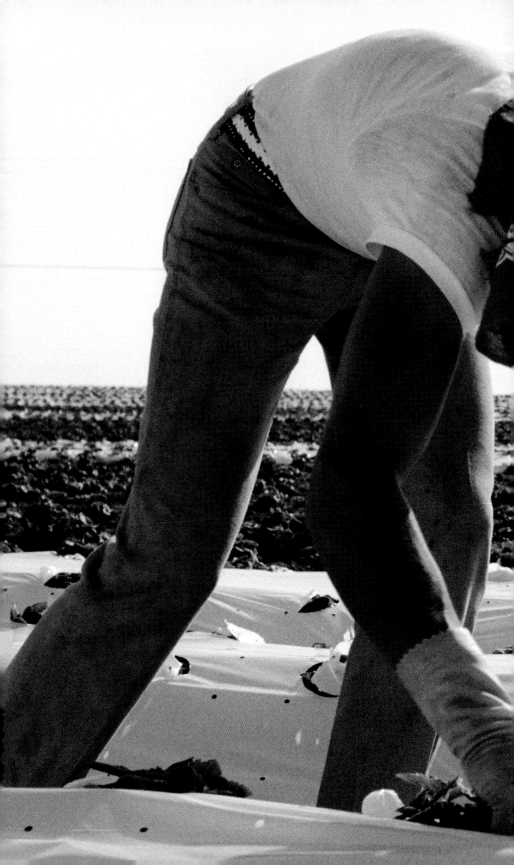

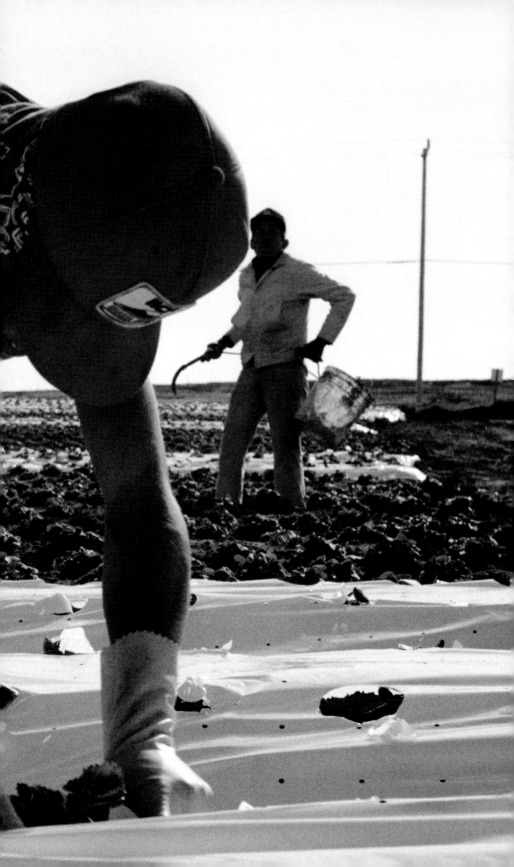

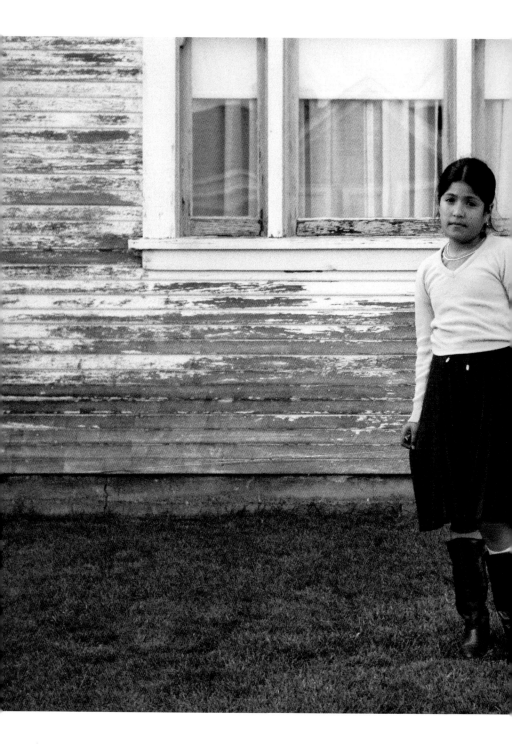

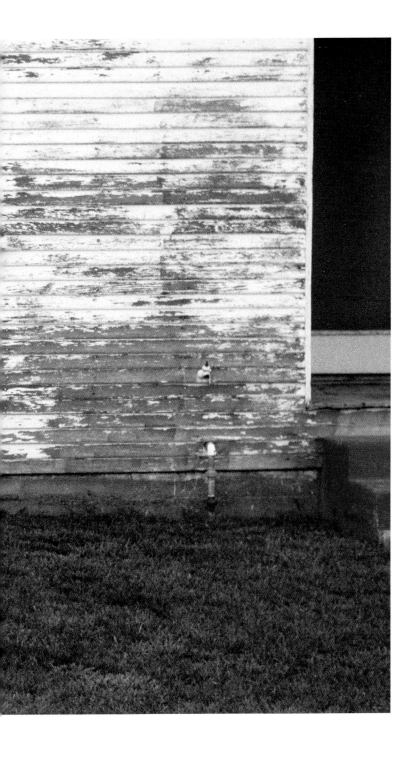

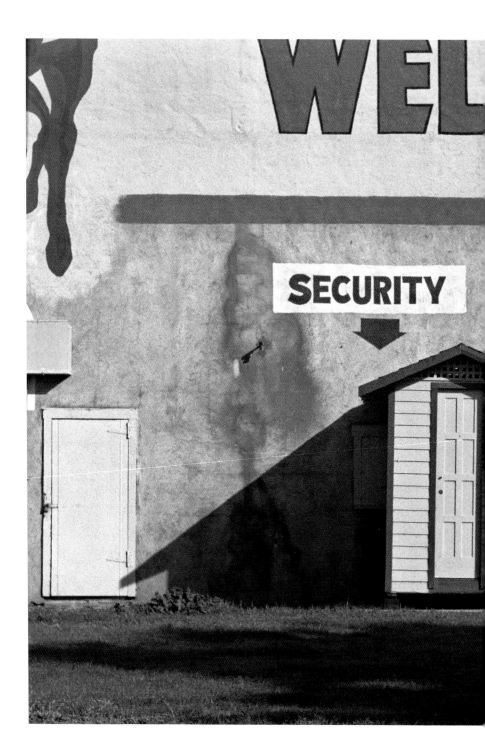

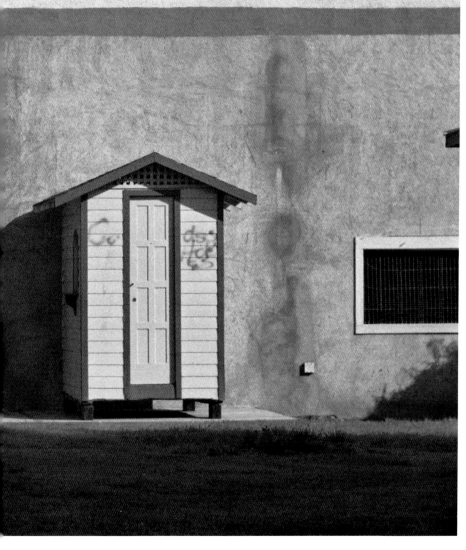

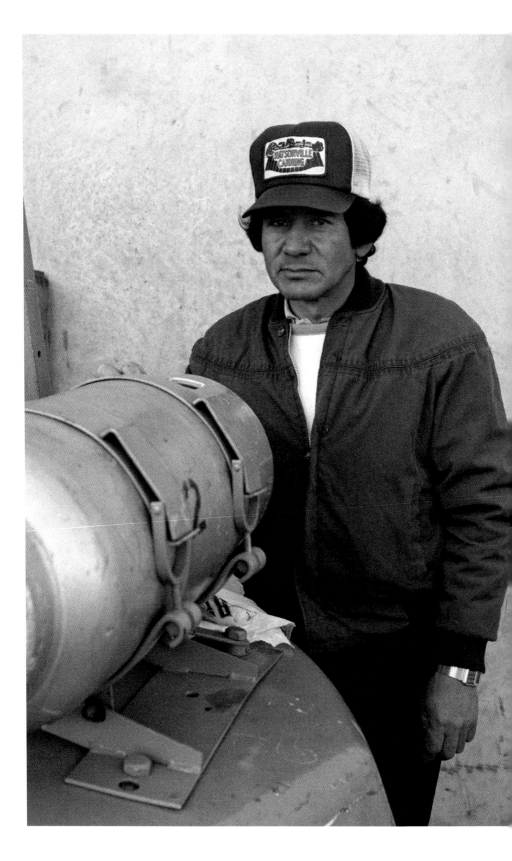

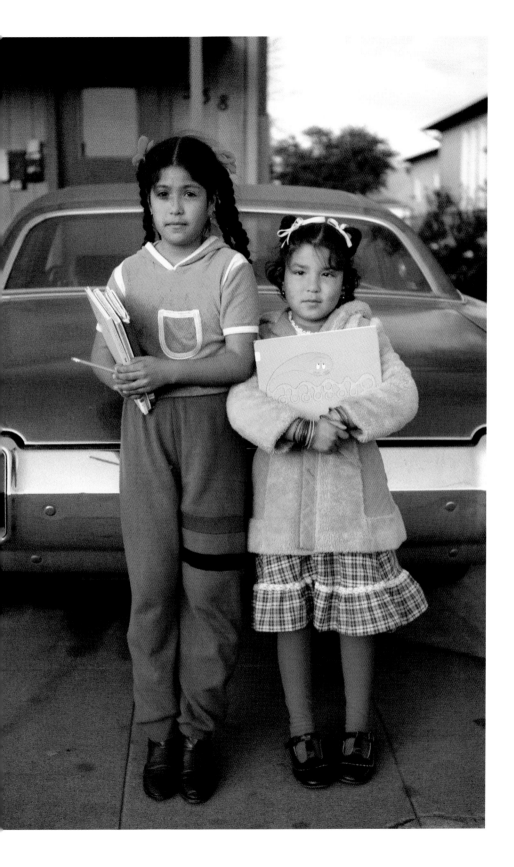

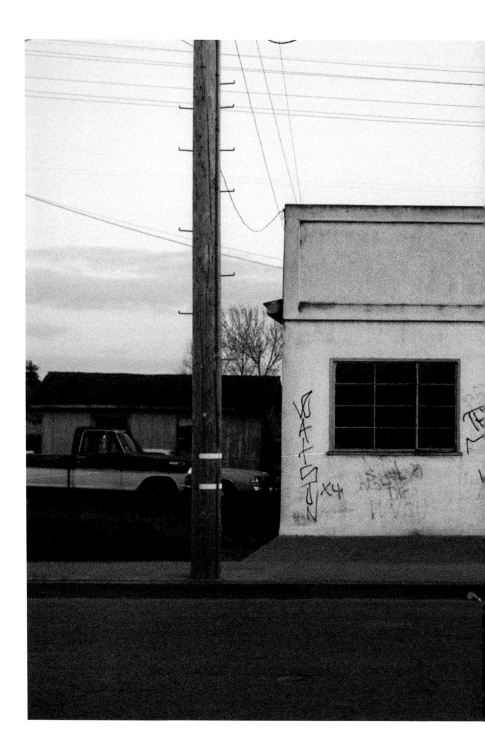

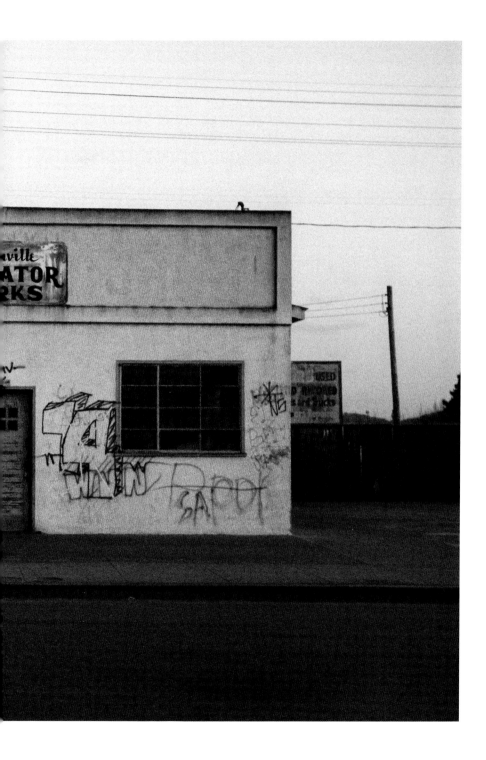

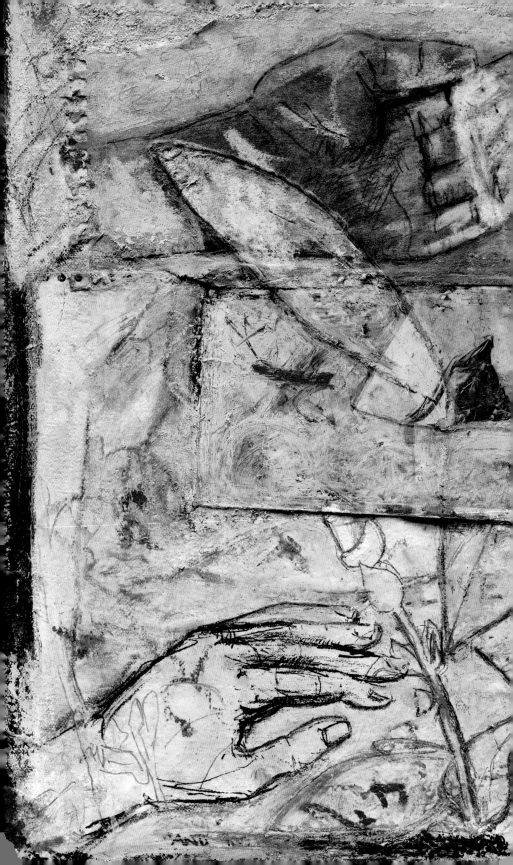

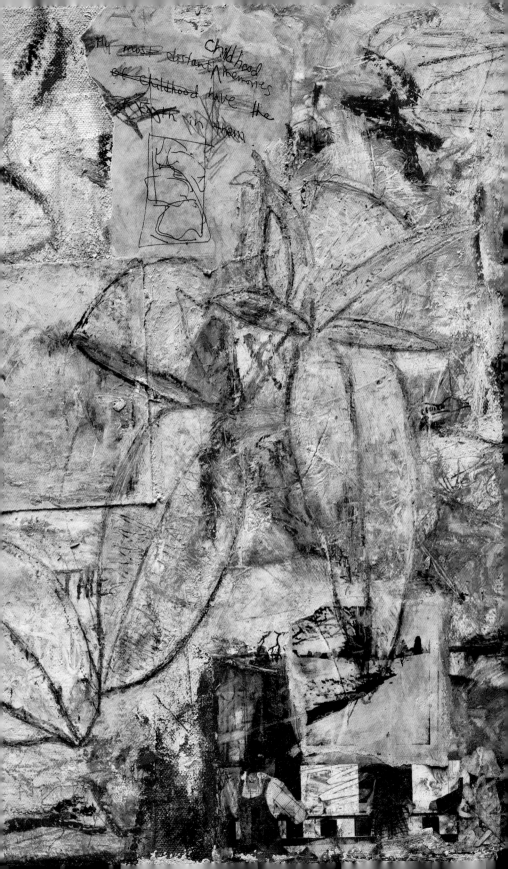

My most distant childhood
of childhood have the
light in them.

Redlands, California, 1978

The day Angie turned twenty (her birthday was May 9, 1958, the same day Hitchcock's *Vertigo* was released) she got behind the wheel of our beat-up formerly white, now rust-colored 1966 Ford Galaxie 500 and, with her cannery money under the seat, we set out together across the desert, heading east into the sun. A hundred thirty years ago settlers found gold and commandeered California from Mexico. We both grew up there like none of that had happened, and now we were leaving it all behind, following the path of the old railroads that brought people west, but we were going the other way. Blasting an eight-track Tornadoes tape, we headed east through Pacheco Pass, then south, carving up the heart of the San Joaquin, and stopped in Redlands to say goodbye to Dad. I wanted to spend the night in familiar air, with the sounds and smells of the place enveloping me in a comforting layer of nostalgia.

Though he didn't seem lonely, I figured Dad had been mostly alone all this time, lost in his thoughts of a history he couldn't control. Over dinner at the International House of Pancakes (newly remodeled) I sat with Dad and Angie in our favorite booth and reminisced about Mom and Mexico City and how the Giants lost the '62 World Series on Willie McCovey's hard liner right to second base; so close, but no glory for the Giants and the great number forty-four on that sad day. We'd followed the game even though we were in Mexico then. Back in San Francisco, Dad's friend Santiago listened on the radio and called in the highlights by phone. Dad smashed the receiver with a golf club when he heard the news. "Remember how I got over it?" he asked, looking straight at Angie and then at me. "I told you there was always next year for the Giants and for you. It's a life lesson. That's how I did it. Timing is everything in baseball, but you always have to look ahead. I don't do that so much any more because for me the future is now. There's not that much time left. You can't know the future; all you can do is imagine it, and what I imagined is gone. My point is this—there's so much in life we can't control. It's better to be in the moment and remember the past, you know, like how a photograph just captures the present and everything that happened before and after just disappears. The only thing left is the moment."

The syrupy smell shot me back to when I was eleven and eating off the kids menu in the same booth by the window. The echoes of a truck coming in hard off the Interstate resurrected those motherless years in the little house off the orchard with Dad and sometimes Addie. Those days of insecurity, of wondering when or if we would ever see Mom again, had held me upright like a pillar. It's why I wanted to be a photographer, to see what I couldn't see and understand the impenetrable density of our past.

Dad was in a pretty good mood that evening, considering all he had lost—his wife was gone and his kids had both moved away—in the span of recent memory. I attributed his reserved clarity and humor that evening, his willingness to engage, to our brief visit. He liked it that we were leaving on an adventure and he liked Angie right away, though they didn't see eye-to-eye on anything. She tried to draw him out, telling him what it feels like to study algebra after a day of bending over picking strawberries one-by-one, and asking probing questions about Mom and Addie and what happened to them. "Listen up, Mr. Dave, I spent a lot of time eavesdropping on Kip and Addie and I know something's up. It's not a very nice story."

I was wobbly because I could tell that Dad had something on his mind, something he wanted to say to me after years of holding it all inside. He was about to explode. As usual, his thoughts were filtered by his intellect, and he sighed like a tired professor explaining something to bored students for the millionth time, hoping they would finally get it. "We all want to understand the past, I write about that sometimes, you know. I think that's why Kip loves to look at the world through that little lens of his. It focuses things; that's always been important for him." He addressed me directly for the first time in the conversation. "Kip, I know you can find joy in those little instants where light and life just happen to come together. I wonder, though, if we can ever find any real meaning there to help illuminate the past? I never figured that out, to tell you the truth."

Then Dad pulled a wrinkled envelope out of his pocket, opened it, and slapped a grainy, yellowing snapshot on the table, a faded picture of Mom and Addie at Drakes Beach, out near the tip of Point Reyes, a family favorite as kids. Mom was smiling in a chiaroscuro black and white. The overhead sun had etched her features into a pattern of circles and triangles on paper, punctuated by wisps of hair that whipped across her face in the wind. Addie was running backwards into the waves, her hair lit up by the sun. Her antics stole the show for the photographer (Dad). She'd almost danced and twirled her way out the top of the frame in a blur of exuberance, unable to hold still for the camera. "You keep that one," Dad said pensively. He committed the image to memory one last time before handing it over.

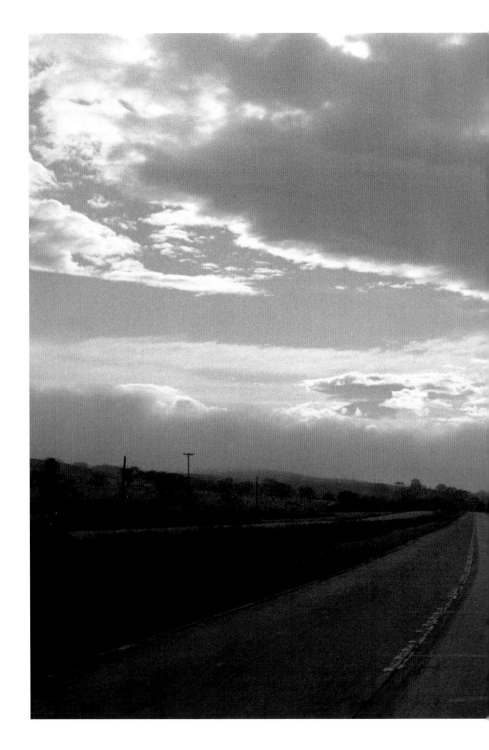

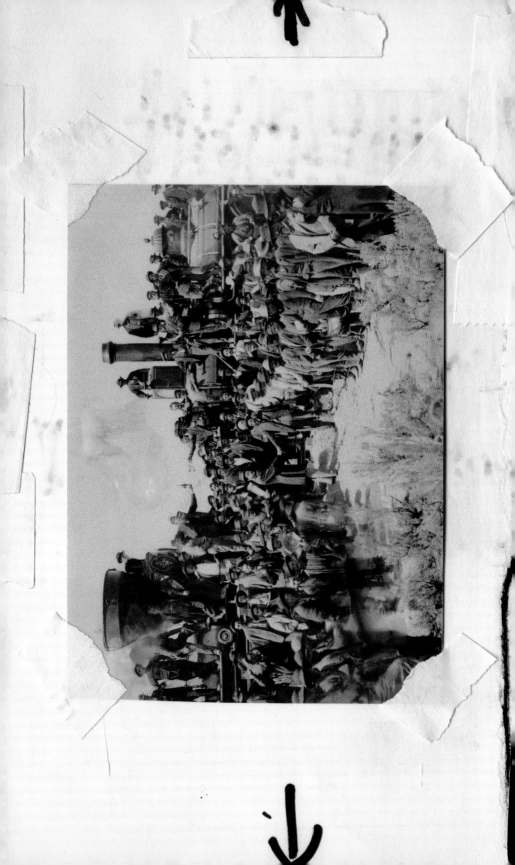

FAR MORE

REMARKABLE IN

~~THE~~ LIGHT

OF MEMORY

TIME

"That's the smile I fell in love with." He started slowly. "Your mother was a tough nut, really hard, and the only other person I ever loved other than my children and my parents. We both had a lot of shit to carry when we met. And I can't even speak about the war. That destroyed my mind before I ever learned to think for myself. But if I learned one thing in the Ardennes, it's that people go to war to be seen. That's about it. The big guys want to be seen and the little guys go through hell and back for them. And when it goes wrong, the big guys are invisible and the little guys end up crazy or dead. The big guys make a profit and it keeps happening again and again. It's just business.

"As for Jess, she lost both her parents before she was fifteen; you know that, Kip. Her mom Dorie died when she was a baby. The flu got her, same with about 50 million other people that year. She never knew her mom. And she rarely saw her father, your grandpa James. They lived in Nanaimo, and he was always gone for days or weeks at a time, working on a steamship that travelled up and down the Inside Passage, hauling freight and passengers from Vancouver and Nanaimo up to Prince Rupert and Ketchikan. Jess was always left behind with the neighbors."

Dad stopped and looked down at his plate, swallowed a few quick bites, and slowly shook his head as the pain sunk in. "The Olsens were missionaries from Idaho who came up to the island to convert the natives." He waited a beat and then went on. "They even took Jess to church with them to expel that 'Jew blood' she inherited from her mother. When she was with them she prayed to their god at dinner and again before bed. She felt abandoned by her father, so she accepted another family as her own. Then one day her father didn't come home. His ship hit a shoal off Gravina Island, and he drowned trying to save a Tlingit child who fell out of the lifeboat. The water was just too cold and they both died. Because there was no one else to take care of Jess, the Olsens took her in full-time, and she lived with them a few more years. She hated it. Her only comfort then was her best friend, a beautiful coon cat that lived outside and hunted mice and squirrels around the neighborhood." Dad rubbed his eyes and looked out the window at the cars speeding by on the highway.

"One day the cat killed a bird and left it on the back steps for Jess. Mrs. Olsen—she loved the songbirds in the trees, thought they were closer to Christ than any of God's other creatures—caught the cat and drowned it on the spot, did it in the laundry tub, left it there for the other birds to see. When Jess found out, she was heartbroken and never got over it. She started acting out: smoking, drinking, sleeping around, racing motorcycles, anything she could think of to get their attention.

"And then she ran away from home when she turned seventeen, ended up toughing it out on the streets in Vancouver until the police sent her back to Nanaimo. The cat's name was Kip. When you came along she named you Kip to remember that old cat she loved so much."

I was silent, stoic. Angie was bent over, shaking her head and hyperventilating. She leaned her head on my shoulder, caught her breath, blinked, and asked Dad in an overly angry tone, "What about Addie—your daughter—how did she peel off the straight and narrow?"

I held up the picture of Mom and Addie, looked at it again for half a second, and stuffed it in my pocket. Dad looked away, shook his head and slowly blew the air from his lungs, like a kid trying to start up a good gum bubble. "She's our daughter, and all I can say is that there was never a clear path for her, or Kip for that matter." He looked at me and looked away. "I know we often tried too hard to be different, to live independently in a world where independence is a day when everybody blows things up. Our family album is full of beautiful pictures from the beach, but none of them tells the real story. Addie knew Jess better than anyone else in her last few years. They tried to take care of each other. You need to ask her if you want to know her side of it. You know, just because someone tells you your mom's dead doesn't make it true. You have to verify the facts for yourself."

The three of us sat and sipped our coffee, winding our conversation back slowly to baseball. Then we went home together for the last time (I didn't know it then) and agreed to keep in touch the old-fashioned way, sending each other the most essential news by postcard.

As we crossed the country, heading east for New York City, Angie and I saw the mountains rising golden green in the evenings and the endless plains reflected a pinkish brown. We stopped from time to time to pick dandelion blooms by the side of the road and blow the seeds to kingdom come, like Addie and I had done when we were kids. Five days later we eased the smoking Galaxie onto the Delaware Bridge and crossed over the river from 95 to the New Jersey Turnpike, heading north through a forest of chemical plants shooting fire into the night sky. This reminded me of L.A. on a good day, so I prayed that my sister was somehow okay among the thieves and goblins of a Southland summer.

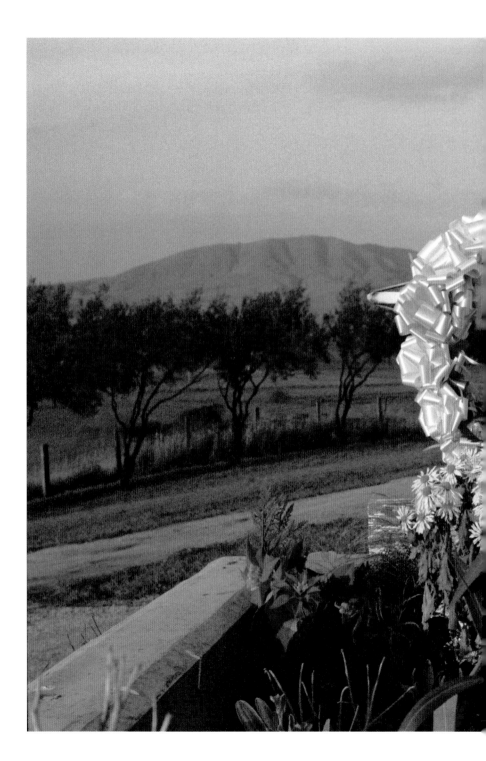

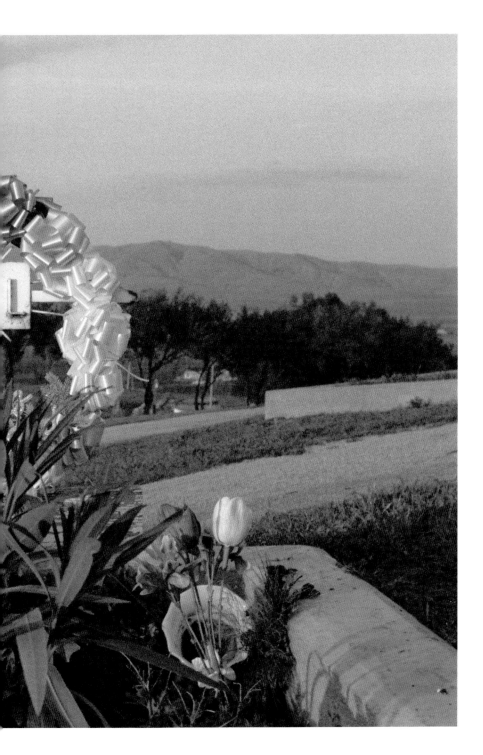

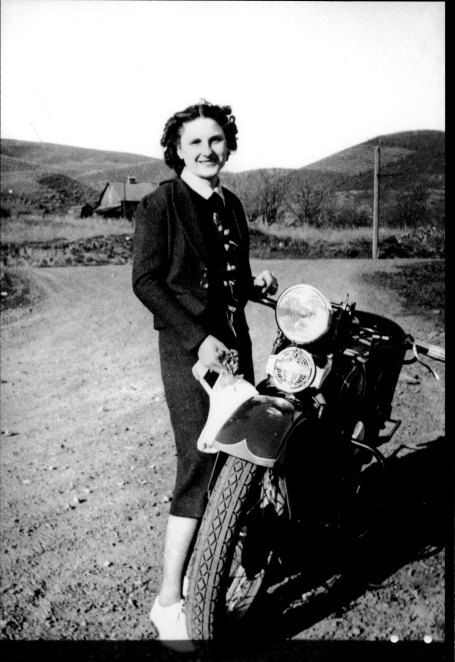

New York City, 1979

We were definitely on the same wavelength from the start and learned to live on very little. We used the sewing machine money to help buy the Galaxie, drove it to Manhattan for the cost of gas and some cheeseburgers, and then sold it to a guy leaving for Colorado. We made a profit of exactly sixteen dollars and thought we were really smart. We were flush as far as I was concerned.

But we were homesick too, so we went for a walk and sat on a bench at the edge of Tompkins Square Park. It wasn't helping. "Kip, remember when you told me about your dream...about going through the arcade in Santa Cruz and coming out on the street in Manhattan? We've done that. We've come out the other side, we're here, but we don't really know what we're looking for. I mean, where's the poem? This isn't Madison Avenue or some other fancy place, that's for sure," Angie said, looking up to spot a skinny kid in tight jeans tagging the call box across the street with a fat marker. "You asked me, 'Why are we here?' So let's think about it for a minute. You know your dad's family is from New York, right? So this place has to be connected to them somehow. Right? They probably lived in this neighborhood. Check. Your dad told us that his dad was born in New York and your great-grandfather came here in the nineteenth-century from Russia or Poland or some other frozen place like that. Check. Where did he live when he came to this country...your grandfather's dad? Is that what you're looking for? Is that what your dream's about? It's taking you back in time, obviously, back to where your ancestors lived."

"What are you going on about?" I asked, stumped by how philosophical she had become all of a sudden. Angie didn't stop to answer. She just stood up and starting jogging south on Avenue A, or Avenue (of the) Assholes, which was a pretty good nickname I overheard in the grocery. She was on a mission, which reminded me of how she'd skipped across the street in Santa Cruz, full of energy, purpose, and longing for the freedom of her childhood.

I was thinking about Angie and how we'd known each other for more than four years. I wasn't alone anymore and it meant something that we worked together to figure things out. I wanted to spend some time taking photographs (that's really why I came to New York) but I wanted to know how we were going to get work to survive. Plus, I was scared. I knew this city chewed up kids and spit them out everyday. It wasn't a very practical idea

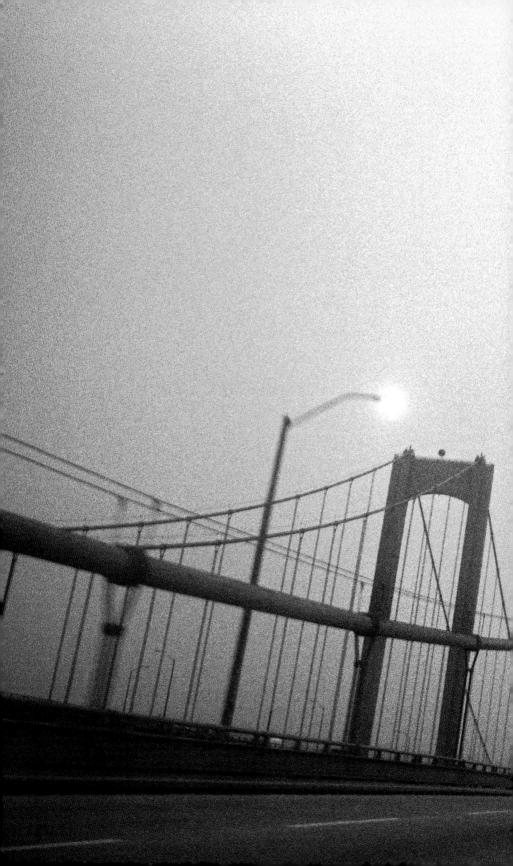

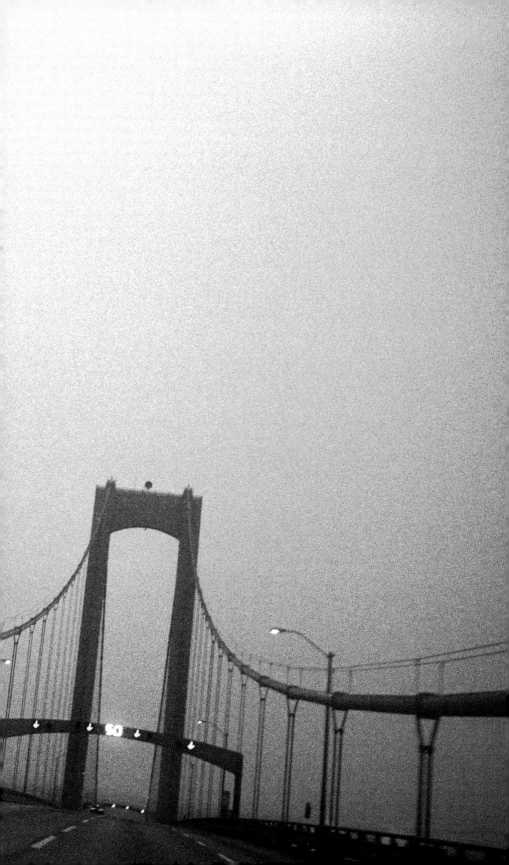

for us to just show up here without a plan, but there was a good side to it too. We were gone from home, emigrants like our ancestors, looking for a better life.

First we moved into a railroad flat on Avenue A, between 3rd and 4th, a stone's throw from the Most Holy Redeemer Church, which had been on the same spot since 1844 or something. This was the only place we could find that didn't require a reference from my employer, who didn't even exist. I got some leftover paint from a construction site and fixed it up a bit, but this place never did pass the smell test. There were two rooms lined up one behind the other and a bathroom in the back, brick walls and one window that looked out onto a heap of garbage. We could pay by the month with no lease, so that was good, but it was impossible to sleep at night because of all the noise. So we'd sit up late swapping stories, like at the Flats.

"Once in L.A., when I was about seven, some older white kids threw mud at me at the pool," Angie told me one night. "They went after me and all my friends like that, didn't want us there. We got scared and ran away. Hey, listen to the sounds out there…humming…screaming…crying. This shit seems to follow us around."

I held my breath, actually stopped breathing for what seemed forever. "Uh…. Well, you're a good listener, so listen to me for a minute. Did I really come all this way because of some stupid dream that's not even real? Did I come here because of some horoscope I read on the back of cereal box? I don't think so. What's real is that we're here together for the first time trying to make a go of it. And we don't know anybody but dopers…and we don't have work…and we're going to run out of money super fast if some douche-bag relator doesn't take it from us first. Damn, Angie, I'm scared we're not going to make it."

"I'm worried too, what do you think? We can always turn back if we get lost, you know, go back to Califas to work the cannery line. That's a normal summer for me. This is different and new and we need to make the best of it, check it out, you know."

A motorcycle screamed through the window, the decibel level rising to the equivalent of a 727. Angie stopped and turned to look me over; her sanguine eyes wouldn't belie her real feelings. She was looking through me and didn't have much more to say. I knew she was excited to be gone from California, but that place—far away now—was still home. Our families (a safety net of sorts) were there, which is why we were here. It didn't make much sense.

Alphabet City was filled with people who'd been hurt before and came here to get over the pain, to turn it into something else. We met actors, artists, and photographers in the bars and interesting musicians in the coffee shops. Writers mixed with addicts to create a nonstop play-within-a-play vibe that never quit. Charlie, the guy in the flat below us, played drums for a "Neo-Stockhausen quartet" (his words), making sounds that were as abstract as some of the best paintings we saw at the Museum of Modern Art. We often went out with him for breakfast (this never happened before noon). He introduced us to a good diner on the corner of 6th and Second Avenue, where you could get eggs and toast with potatoes and coffee for two dollars and ten cents plus tip. "I want 'em cooked hard, break the yolk, flip 'em over, and cook 'em hard, really hard, I'm from Kansas, come on, cook 'em some more," he would shout at Rudy, the exhausted cook who'd been there since four in the morning.

After breakfast we sometimes stopped at the Candy Store, where Charlie would whisper to the man behind the counter for a dime bag—his ability to pay depended entirely on tips from last night's session—which he would roll up meticulously and share with us later in the day if we were all hanging around together on the stoop. Some nights we could hear him playing midnight solos in the park, beating on an old drum set or trash cans, birthing sounds that could be mistaken for heavy traffic on the Avenue. "That's just the point," he explained, shouting with total conviction. "After John Cage, there's nothing at all left to do but shut the fuck up and listen to what's around you."

A few months later we were standing around the park watching the show, sweating like crazy in the humid sauna of a late afternoon. "I know where he lived," Angie teased, twisting around to look back over her shoulder. She stopped and waited for me to catch on. "Come on. Follow me."

She was off down the street before I could say anything. Once we got to Houston we crossed and turned right. The sun was hot on the sidewalks and the air was still heating up, turning a pale opaque beige-gray color that signified late summer in New York City. I knew the names of these streets from eavesdropping on conversations between Dad and Grandpa Joe—Essex, Ludlow, Orchard (this always reminded me of Redlands), Eldridge—even though he never talked to Addie and me about that part of his life. Maybe it was something negative from the past. By the time Dad was born, a lot of Jewish families had moved out of the Lower East Side to the suburbs, or better yet, the Midwest. He left when he was just a baby and grew

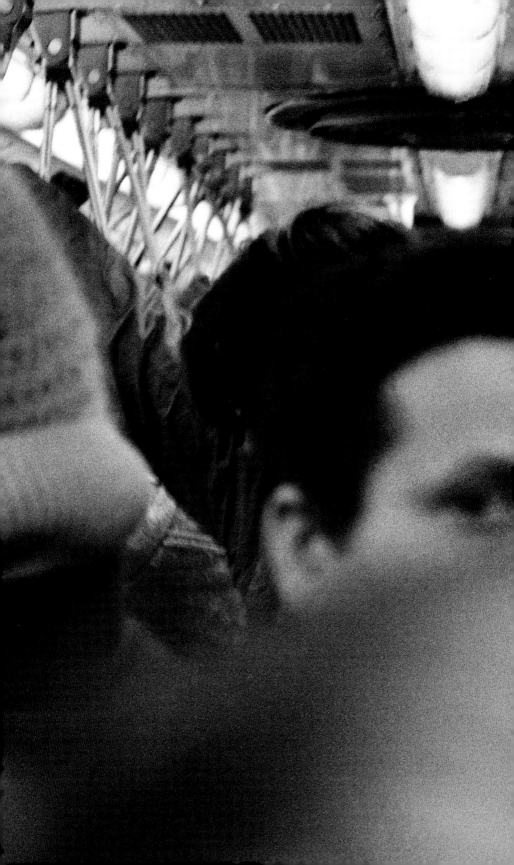

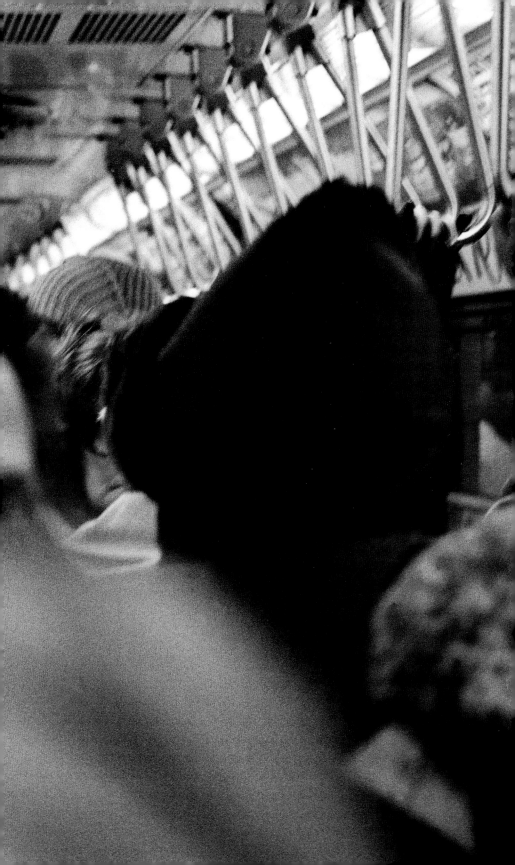

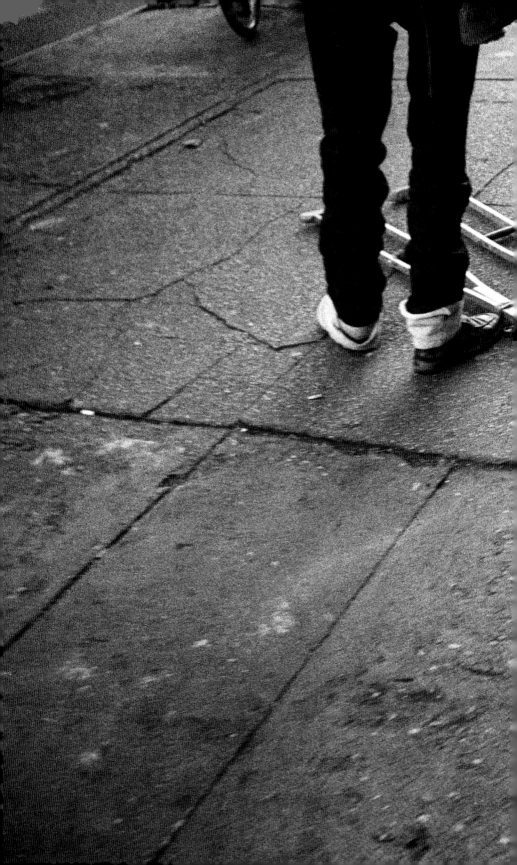

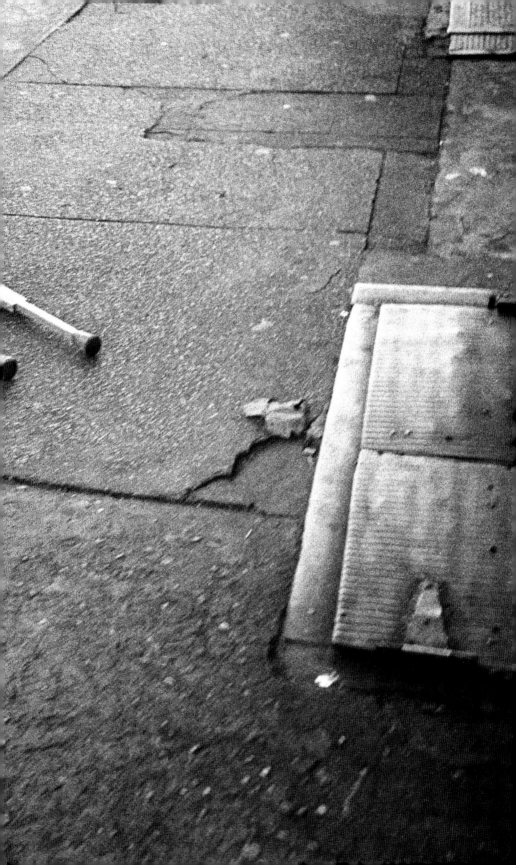

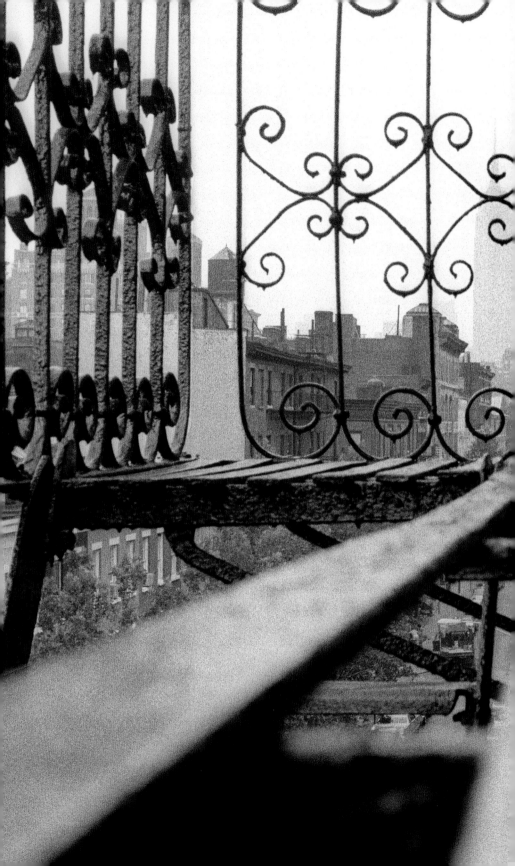

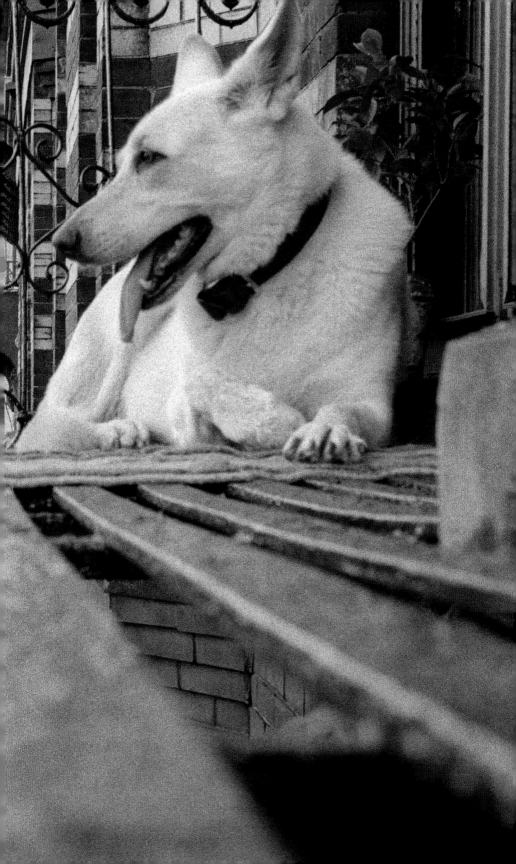

up in Brooklyn, "a subway stop and a world away," as Grandpa Joe told him during one of their conversations.

I felt like this neighborhood was locked up in my DNA. There must be some reason why it felt so familiar. With Angie in the lead, we turned again, walked south on Eldridge and crossed Canal. Her detective radar was turned all the way up; suddenly she stopped, spun, and grabbed my arm, wrenching my whole body around to face the street. "This is it. He lived at 9 Eldridge Street. That's the number, look there, n-i-n-e, nine. It's that place right over there." Angie pointed across Eldridge to a simple bodega selling bread, milk, sandwiches, and candy, along with cheep wine and beer out of a sunken nondescript storefront squatting under a five-story tenement.

I stood on the sidewalk looking up to take in the whole building, which was pretty big, solid brick construction, with steps going up the outside to the fire escapes that dressed the front like a lacy curtain hanging over a hundred years of dirt. "The only thing upgraded is the storefront. Everything else looks the way it did when it was built during the Gilded Age," she said. "All that wealth never came near this community. The Lower East Side is a transitional neighborhood and always was for working class people, mostly immigrants. This is where your great-grandfather landed when he came from Europe. He became a tailor and was married in this building in 1880."

I looked at her like she was from the moon. "How do you know this stuff?"

"I did my research. Listen...it's quiet here...nice...huh," said Angie, who was truly proud of her discovery.

I stood there with my mouth open and eyes dancing between her beaming face and the old storefront. Angie turned me around in a half circle, panning the street to land face-to-face with the big old white barrel-vaulted synagogue opposite, a beautiful building with a circular window that was almost falling down from neglect.

"You know what it makes me think?" she asked pensively. "It was just the same for my dad, you know. He was an immigrant too. Only it was L.A. and not the LES. They're pretty far apart, but not so different, in terms of their experiences. They were both trying to get away from something that was over and make a better life for their families."

The whole thing gave me a chill, even though the temperature was approaching ninety-five, with humidity closing in on three digits. "Angie, really, how do you know all this? How do you know this is where he lived?"

"Come on, I looked it up, it's not rocket science. I went to City Hall and got his marriage certificate. It said he was married to your great-grand-mother on October 1, 1880 and he lived at 9 Eldridge Street. That's it. This is the place."

She kept after me, pushing to explore that dream that steered me to New York in the first place and brought me literally to the doorstep of my past. Sure, it conveyed some new understanding of my own history, but I didn't really get it. What was I looking for in this dreary, overheated place? "You're the smart one. Does it really mean anything in the context of my real life?" I asked Angie later over ice cream.

"I don't know," she said. "You'll have to answer that one for yourself."

Angie was bored and moving toward practical. She missed California and wanted a real taste of the independence she couldn't find among the high-rises and tenements—the high and low—of Manhattan. After awhile she just couldn't stand my uncertainty, so she took all the money she saved working nights at the copy shop on Bleecker and flew back west to L.A., thinking she should get a job at Carl's Jr. or something and finish high school before getting into another debate with me—or anyone else for that matter—about the past.

I went back to Eldridge Street day after day for weeks, then months. It was like that Beatles song "Revolution Number 9," where the number nine gets hammered into your head over and over again and you have no idea what it's about but you know it's supposed to mean something. I never took a single picture. I didn't have any idea what I was looking for. I tried to imagine him there—a young man from another time I never knew—so I walked around and around that block for so long that one day a neighbor got suspicious and called the police.

I tried to explain.

The cop shrugged and told me that his father had grown up right down the street on Canal. "He came over from Puerto Rico after the war. Small world, man," he glared, shaking his head. "Now I'm chasing the next gen-eration of dopers and gamblers down the same fuckin' streets. Hope you find what you're lookin' for, man."

That night I dreamed I entered the old storefront at number 9, but it looked different. I asked if anyone there knew my great-grandfather. An old Chinese man behind the counter told me in broken English that I could find him on the fourth floor, "rear apartment, the one with the blue door." I repeated my great-grandfather's name again slowly, and the old man said again, "I told you, fourth floor, at the back," nodding to the steps

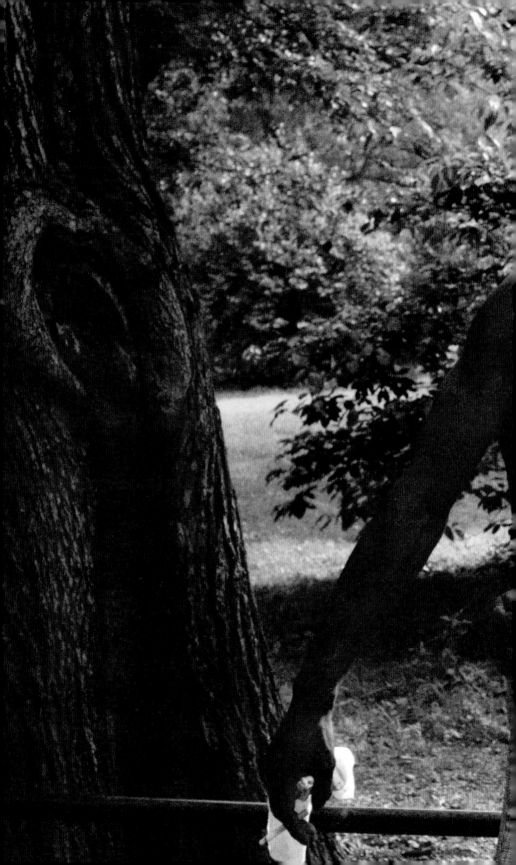

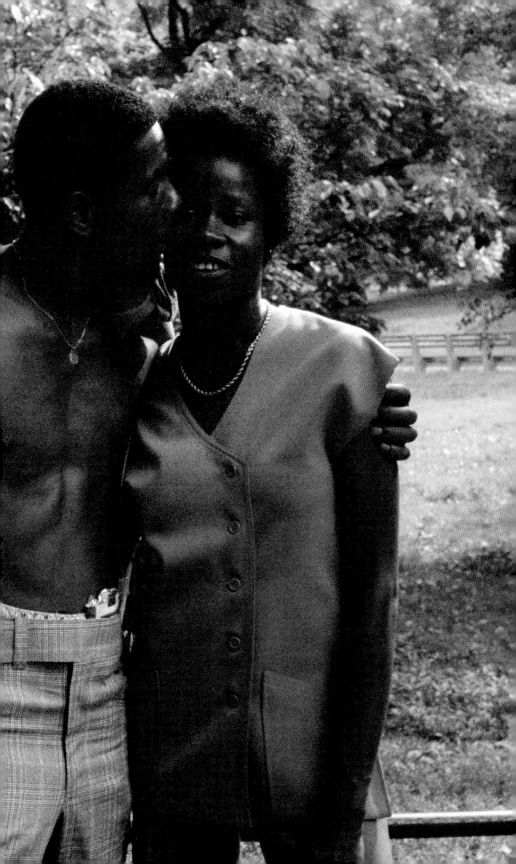

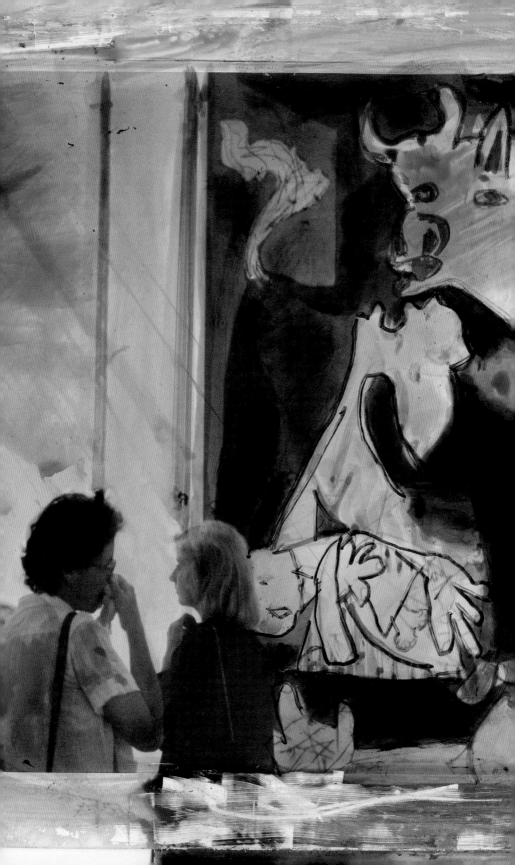

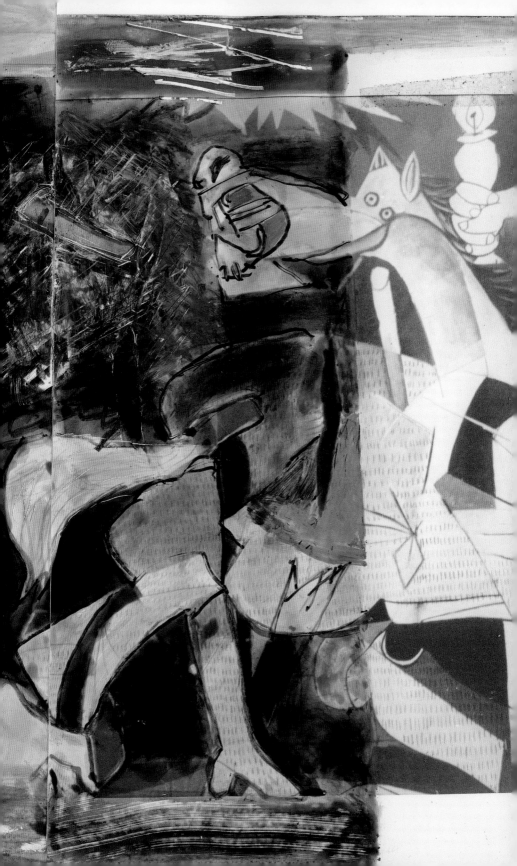

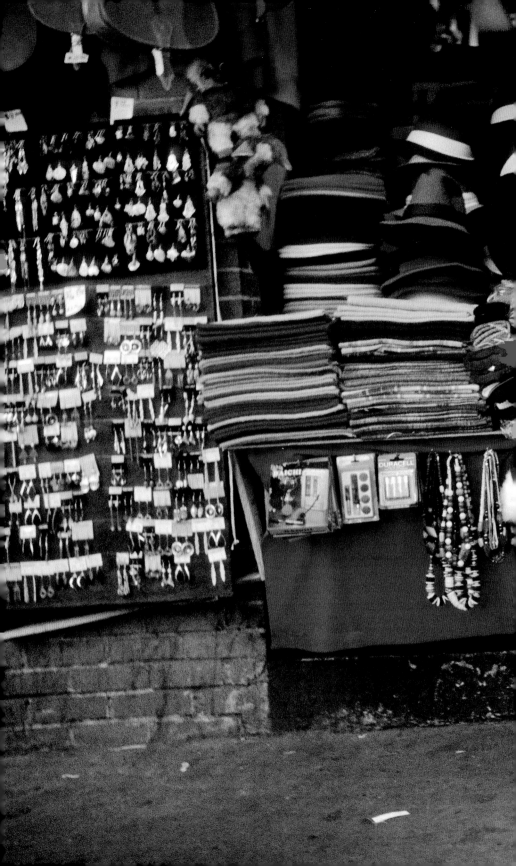

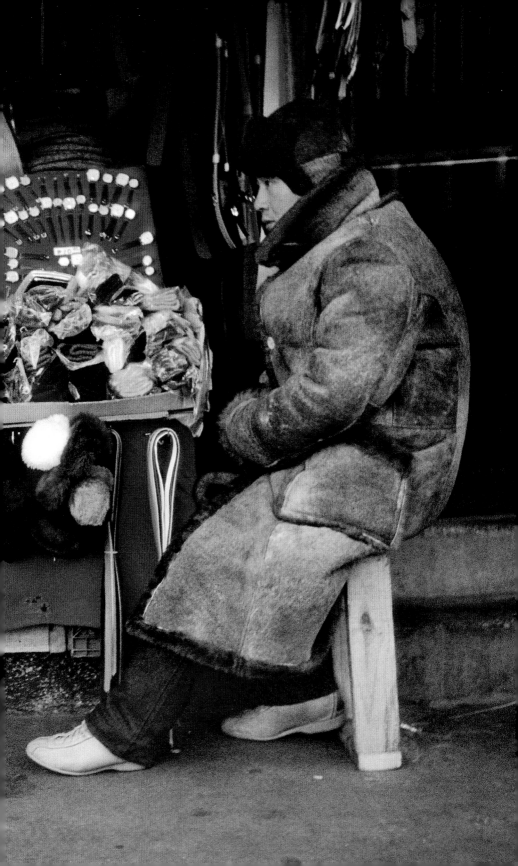

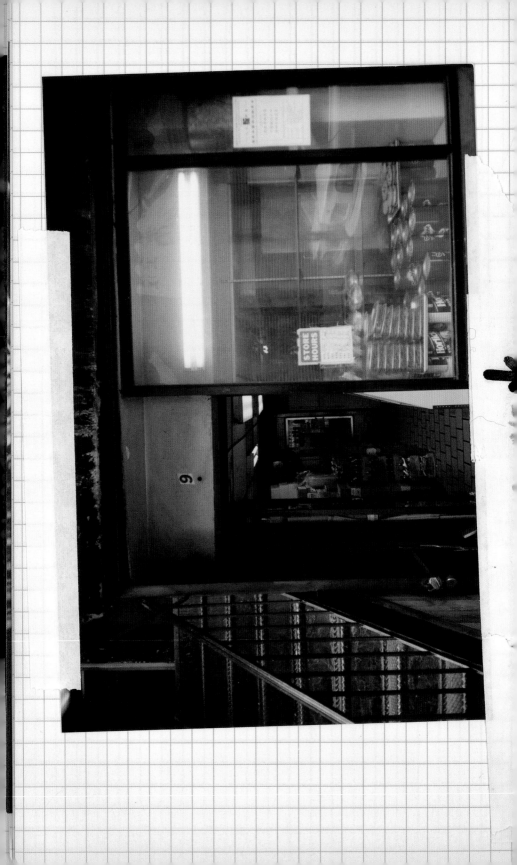

Dream 1 the poem found

FOUND

THE ARCADE

left behind (for emily)

our person to ~~~~ Havi

for a future

TIME

just outside the big shop window. I took the stairs two at a time, flying up to the fourth floor as though I was being lifted on wings right through the window.

I entered his room and there was nothing, it was completely empty except for a small table in the middle and a black notebook filled with short poems. There was no clue about who had written them, just a young man's diary filled with scribbled words.

I woke up, sweating, heartbroken, and alone. It was just a dream and I couldn't read the poems or learn any more about the man who wrote them. I wanted to see him, talk to him, ask him questions about why he left home and came to New York in the first place, but like Dad always said, "Some things you'll never know."

Angie was gone; it was noisy out, cars and buses honking and shouting a familiar dissonant tune. And out of all that noise a cheesy melody congealed from the dust in the alley behind the apartment. The Stones were singing loud and clear from a giant boombox; it woke me up and brought me back to the moment. I got out of bed, looked out through bars on the back window, nothing, stumbled down out front and there's Jeremy, a neighborhood junkie and trash collector who was usually up about this time sitting on the stoop making a racket. He was carrying Keith and Mick down the Asshole, their lyrics fading fast as he shuffled south toward Canal, hoping to pawn a few sentimental words for another fix:

All the dreams we held so close
Seemed to all go up in smoke
Hate that sadness in your eyes
But Angie, I still love you baby
Everywhere I look I see your eyes....

First thing, I put those words on a postcard of the Roosevelt Island Tram—one of our favorite late afternoon stops in the city—and sent it off to Angie.

"Oh god, this is so sappy," she screamed at me through the phone when she got my note. "That song sucks so bad I'm tearing up this card right now. If I ever hear those words again I'm going to Montana or maybe Alaska, where they never play that shit, never even heard of Keith Richards or his stupid problems with girls and dope. I appreciate the thought, Kip, but damn, couldn't you pick a better song?"

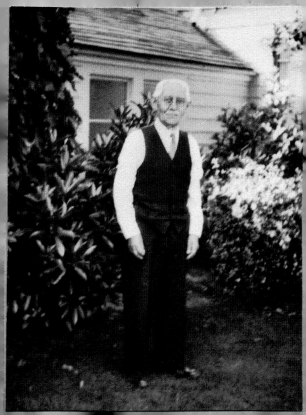

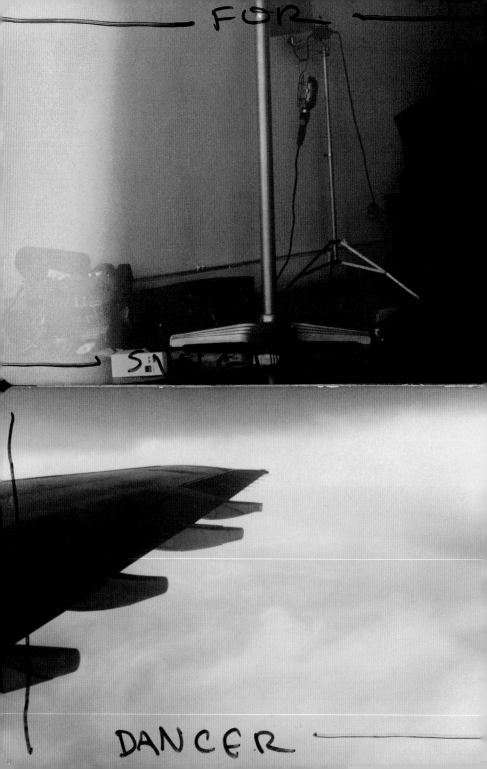

FOR

DANCER

A

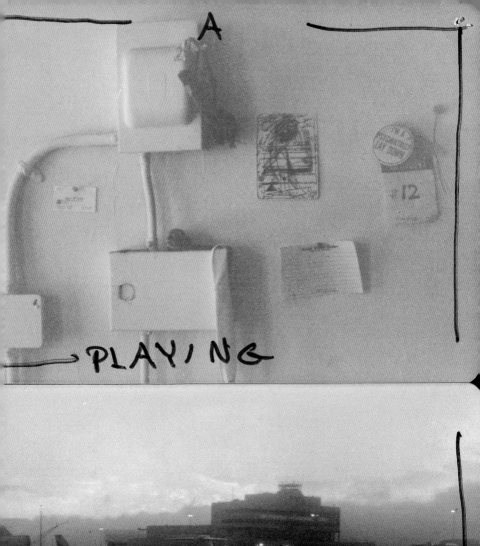

PLAYING

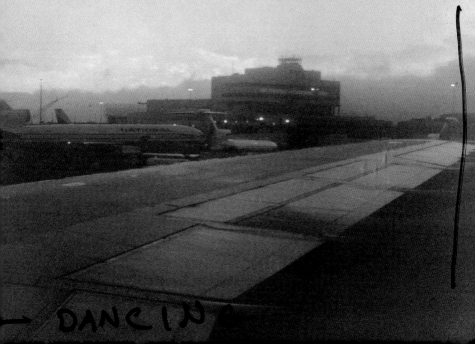

DANCING

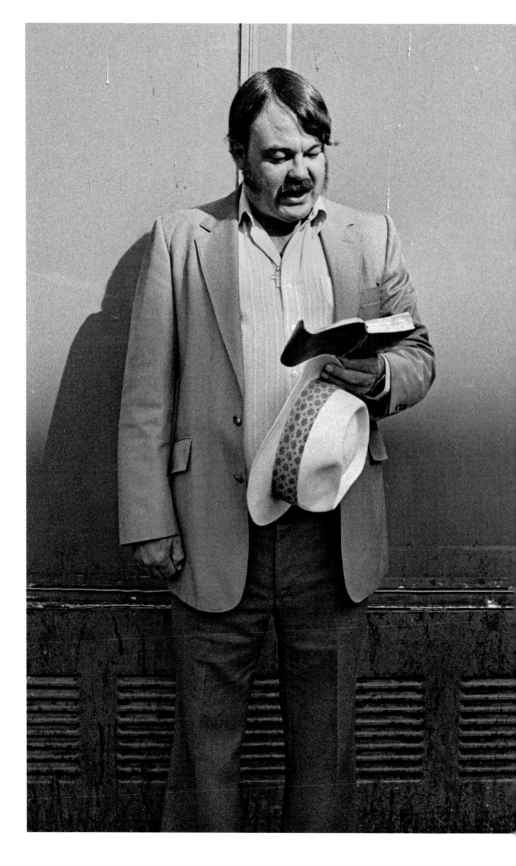

San Diego, 1982

During the time I spent in New York, Addie slowly bottomed out, bouncing from the street to short-term relationships to welfare hotels downtown along the fringe of Bunker Hill. Her letters had become incoherent and her tone was approaching desperate. The last one I received was a warning. The next morning I packed some clothes in my duffle, threw everything else but my camera, film, and a few photos in the garbage, settled up with the landlord, and caught an afternoon flight home to California. When we finally reconnected, Addie could only describe her life to me though a series of smells usually associated with bad luck. A moldy, cat shit, rancid, sharp, aged, stale, rotten, polluted, piss, acrid, acidic, fusty, steamy, roach-infested aroma followed her everywhere. It reminded me of that line from a John Fante novel I once had read at Park Place to put myself to sleep after a long day on the cannery line: "The world is dust, and dust it would become."

A few years back, Addie had written to me in New York, saying she worked in an office as a secretary and everything was stable in her life, but that was a lie. Now she was living just off South Hope Street, where she was squatting with friends. She was so glad to see me back in L.A. that she couldn't let go when we saw each other for the first time in several years. I brought her some confidence and a shadow of family to cling to. As for me, I wanted to be out on the street looking at everything with my camera, still working to figure out what went wrong in our lives. We went for long walks, always skirting the downtown neighborhoods she called home. We crossed over the Los Angeles River into East Los, where the smells were more promising. We sat for hours on bus benches snacking on the cheap tacos and *horchata* I bought on the street to remind myself of Calle Carranza back in Mexico City.

As far as I could tell, all the people who passed by were mostly going somewhere. They appeared either really rich or really poor. The bankers and real estate investors in Lincolns eyed the terrain for opportunity, and the addicts and sweatshop workers stood on corners stooped over from years of abuse, waiting for a bus or a fix. There was nothing in between the two but the LAPD, trolling the streets for trouble in their black and whites. Addie was lucky; she had been in jail only once on a prostitution charge, which she beat. You really couldn't picture the scene with a camera or even describe what was going on there. All you could do was drink it in and piss it out in a language that didn't even exist then.

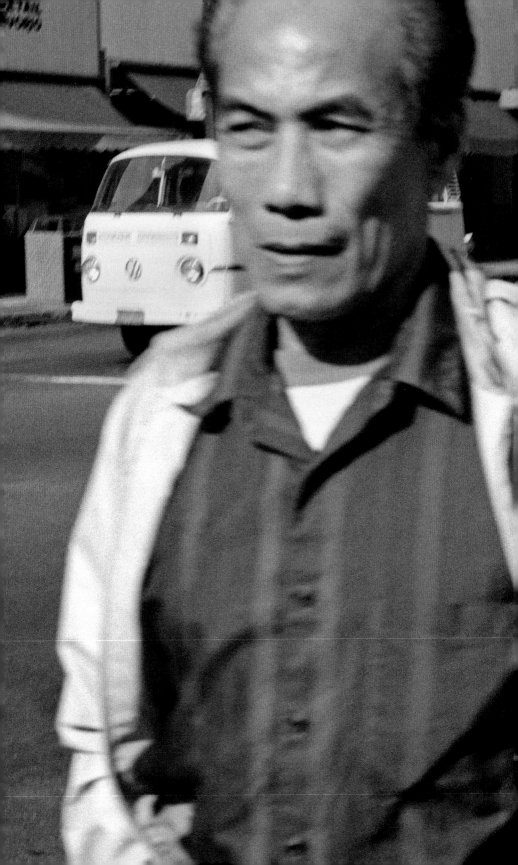

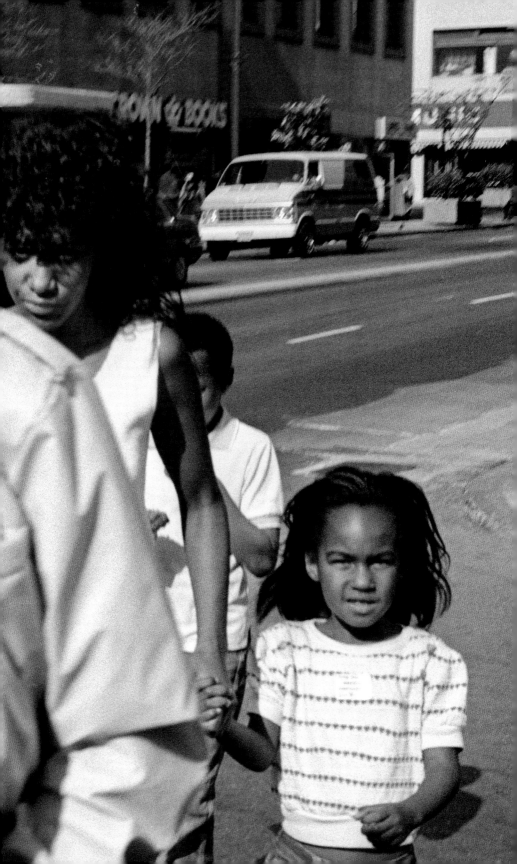

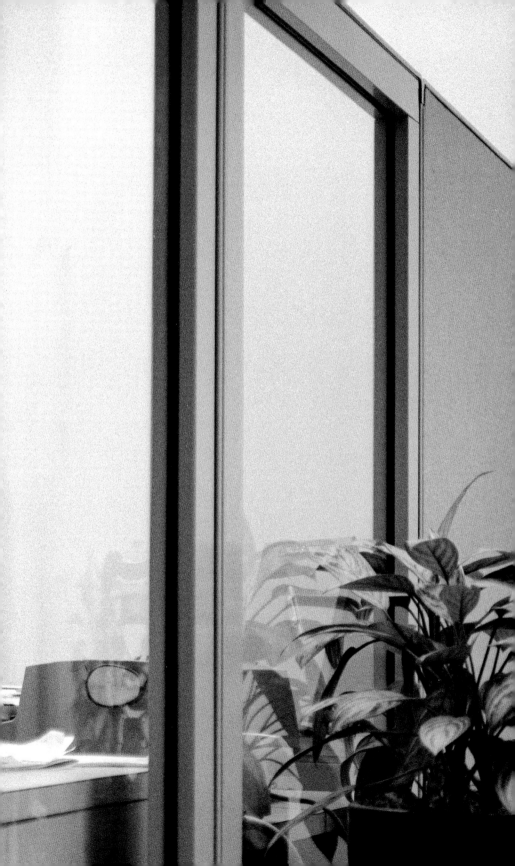

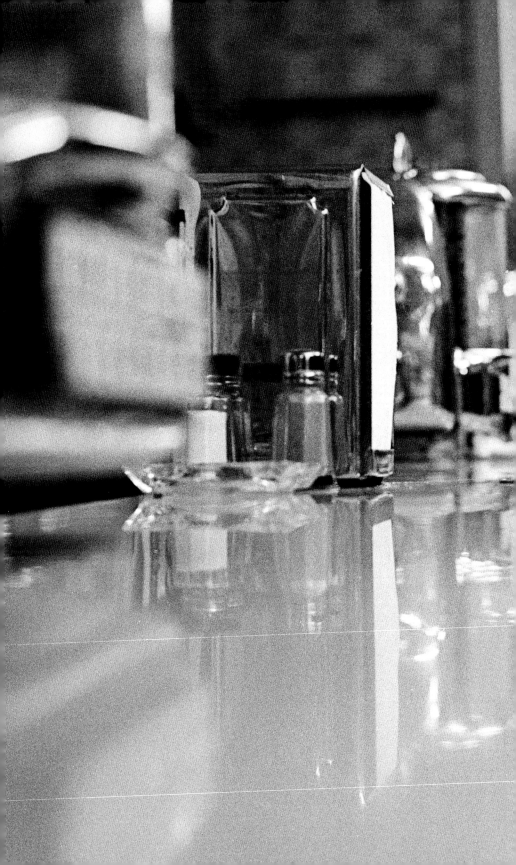

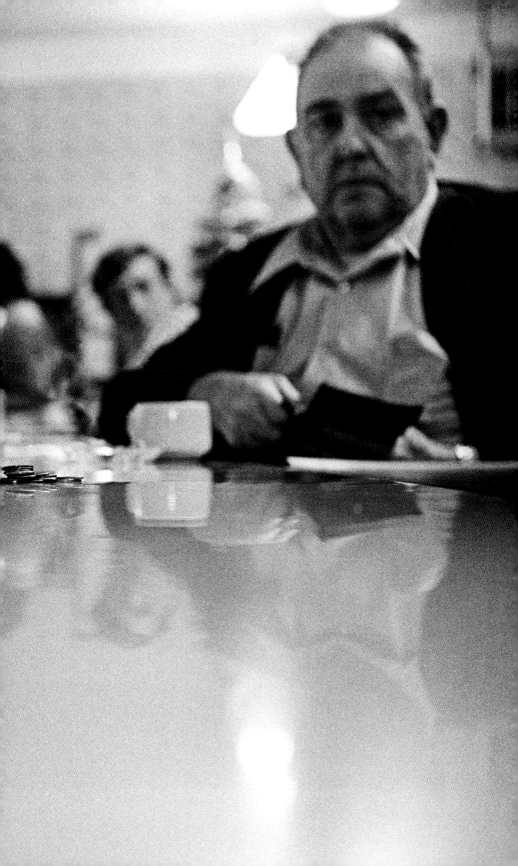

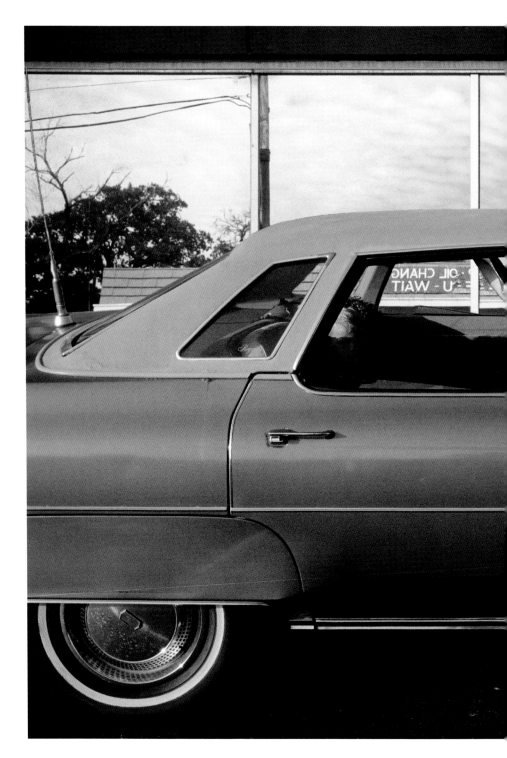

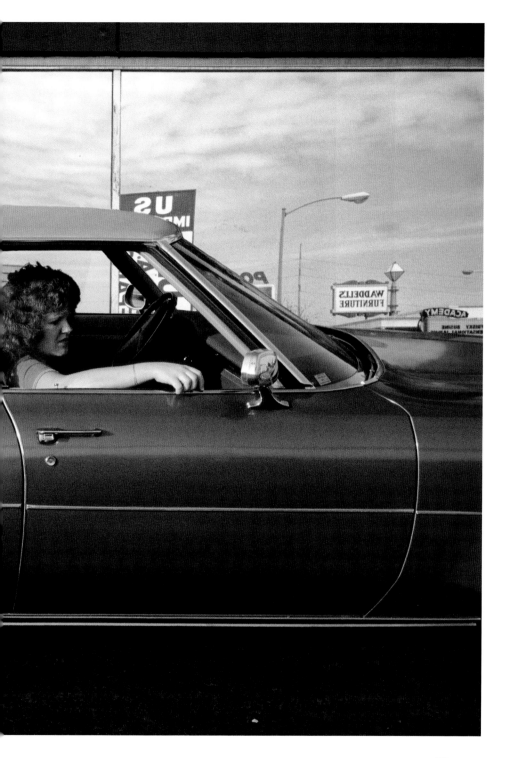

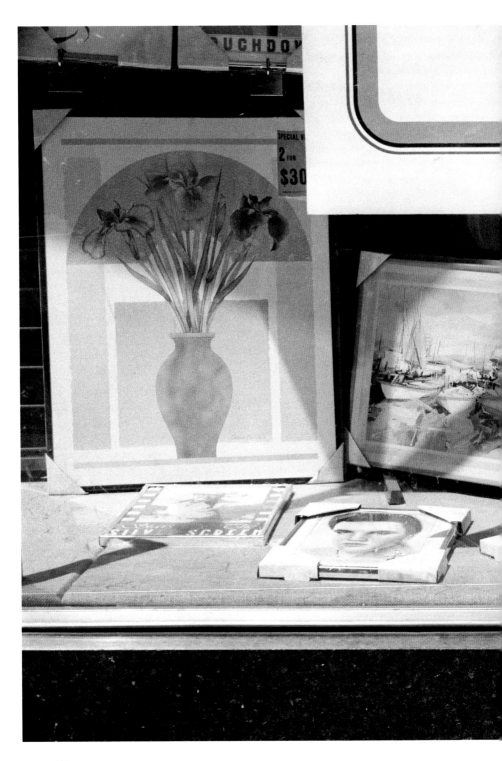

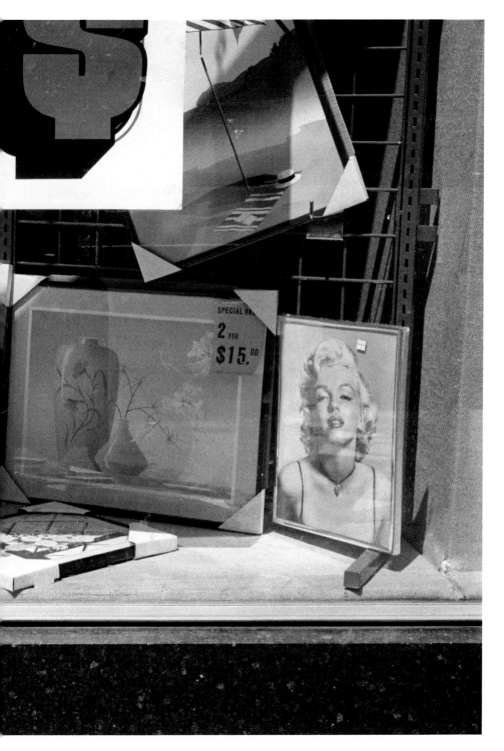

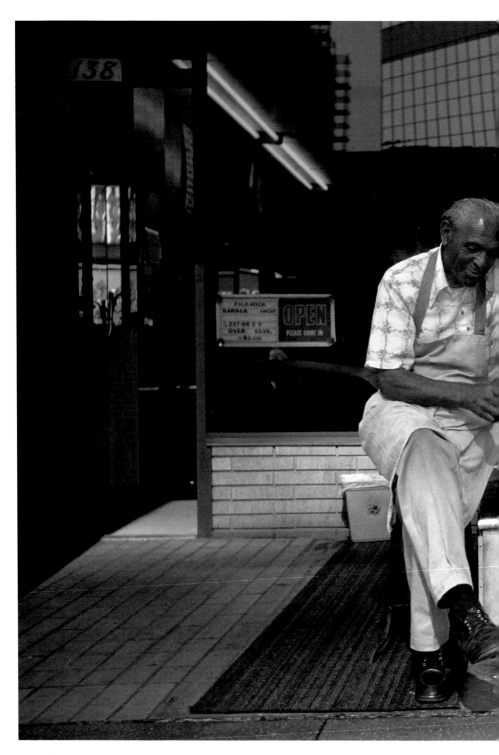

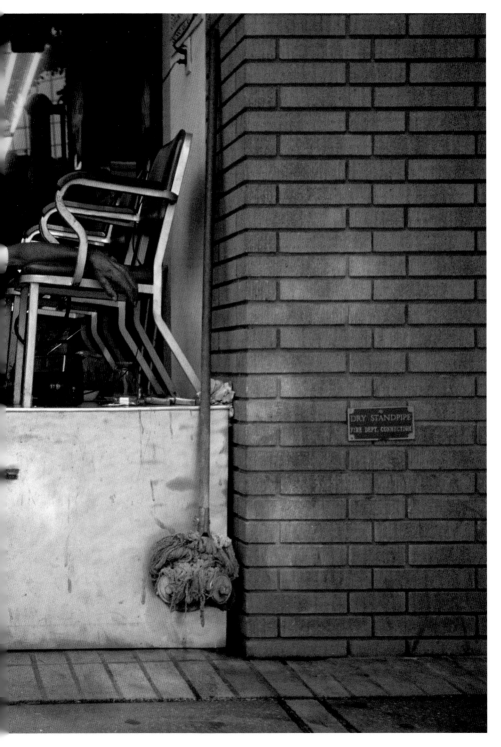

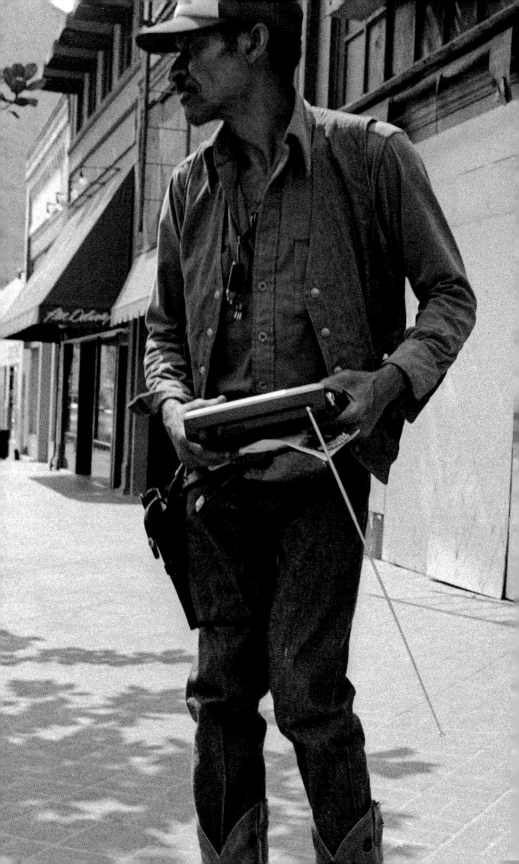

Angie was taking night classes at Fullerton College to get her GED, a half hour bus ride from her apartment in Buena Park, while working days in a warehouse packing flowers that came in from the valley on big refrigerated semis. The only good thing about that job was talking to the drivers, who told her stories of their three-day nonstop speed-fueled runs across the continent, carrying lettuce from the verdant fields of Salinas to the gleaming kitchens of SoHo. One day I hitched down from L.A. for a visit.

"Can you imagine what it takes to grow and ship one head of red leaf?" she asked over coffee at Dunkin' Donuts. "Those are the fields I worked as a kid. Just to raise one lettuce from a tiny seedling warming in the sun to consumption at a New York salad bar, all in one short season, it's mind-blowing we do it all. This is why my family came to California as *braceros* in the sixties. And now they just throw the lettuce in the garbage at the end of a New York lunch. I've been thinking about this a lot since going back to school."

"You know, I worked as a dishwasher for a few weeks in New York. So I'm the one who tossed that shit down the sewer," I responded. "They wouldn't let us take it home."

Angie shook her head. "You have a lot of time to think when you work the fields, you know. A lot of people would think about home and family and politics, but not me. I always liked to look at the plants and get my hands dirty, to understand their cycles and stuff. I know that when you prepare the soil for planting you have to clear out all the invasive plants and bugs, the weeds and shit that take root and push out what you really want to grow for food. And the longer the invaders have been around, the deeper their roots. Sometimes they are really hard to get rid of."

Angie let it slip that she had decided to check out San Diego, in part to get some distance from her parents, who now made a pretty good living from a Mexican bakery they started in Long Beach. We went down together on the bus, holding hands along the way, and the same day we signed a month-to-month agreement on a tiny bungalow off Ocean Beach. The salt air and the endless drone of waves crashing on the beach made it feel right, familiar, a soothing place and a good platform for us both to get back to figuring things out between us. All we had to do was find work and a place in our lives where things flowed in a coherent way. Living by the beach again helped, but San Diego was in transition and you had to have a lot of money to live there; we both knew it was a short-term proposition.

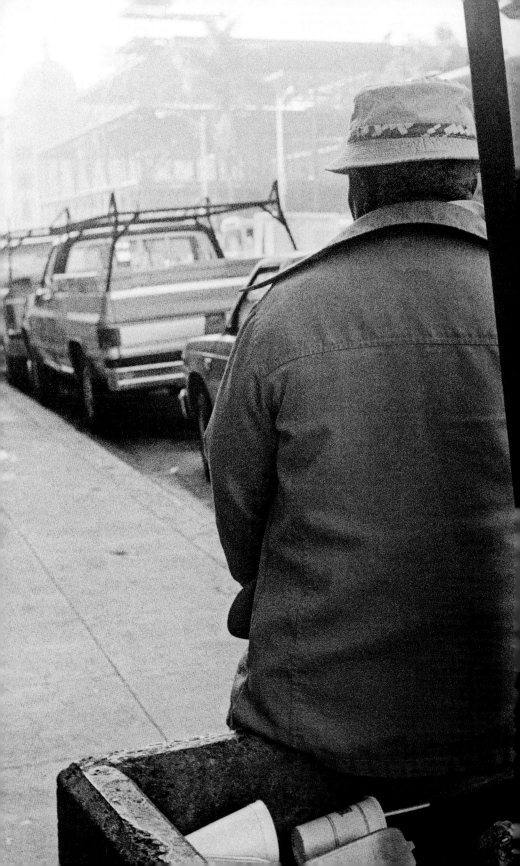

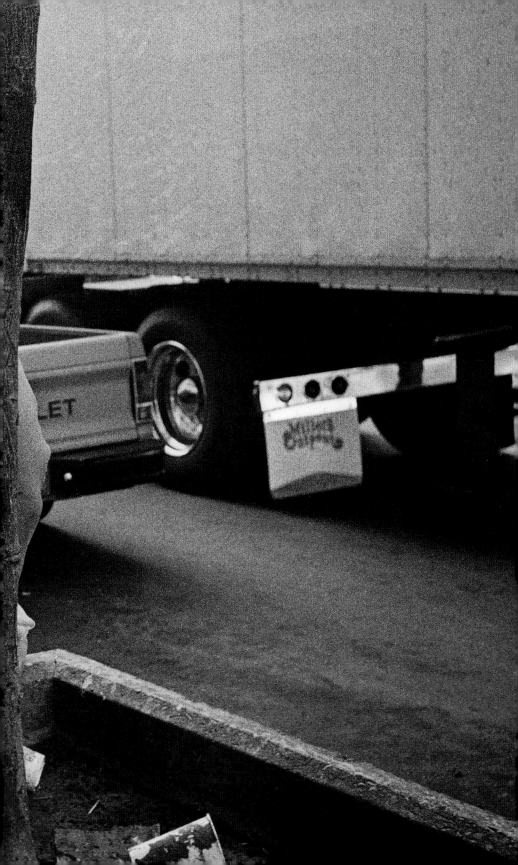

Angie got work in an office and continued with her night classes at the community college. Addie came down from L.A. for a visit and was amused to see us together again, "Just like the good old days in New fucking York." Although she was still scuffling at the edges, she had quit drinking and felt healthier, looking forward to getting up every day and starting out fresh, putting one foot in front of the other, day by day. Addie hadn't seen Angie for years, and when they were together again they hugged and squealed like little girls, something I hadn't seen Addie do since she was in seventh grade; what a feeling that was. She told us she had met a counselor on the street by accident, "From one of those 'help the addict' organizations." Amy convinced Addie to take her life seriously. She taught her that even though she had failed with a lot of personal responsibilities, it wasn't all her doing. She had made a lot of bad decisions, plus there was a long chain of events in our family that made things harder, beginning back in 1918 or even before. And somewhere along the way we had to break that chain or the problems would continue through generations. Addie had to start somewhere, so she quit drinking and doing dope, "Just like that…." She took a deep breath and blew the air out slowly, methodically, like Dad did when he was nervous or exasperated.

They posed together for a photo by the card table in the window, like sisters coming home from school, happy and proud of doing really well on a big test. The light from outside illuminated Addie's face—it was bright and clear like when we were kids—and she looked for all the world like a young Jess at Drakes Beach in the photo Dad gave me. The smile Dad fell in love with was still there in Addie. I went to find the picture, which was one of the few I'd carried with me from Redlands to New York and back. To me it represented a different kind of chain that wound through time and helped link the days and memories of generations. But it held a code that made sense only to the people who lived through those days and carried the DNA from one generation to the next. I shared the image with Addie, who was so much the sprite in the picture and so real and solid in the room with me.

She looked away and handed it back with an awkward glance.

Before she left San Diego, Addie asked us to meet her the following Saturday at Redondo Beach, the same place we ran away to for about ten minutes when we were kids. We agreed on the magic hour before sunset and the same spot at the base of Artesia we both remembered. When Angie and I arrived a week later, we looked out to see Addie in the distance,

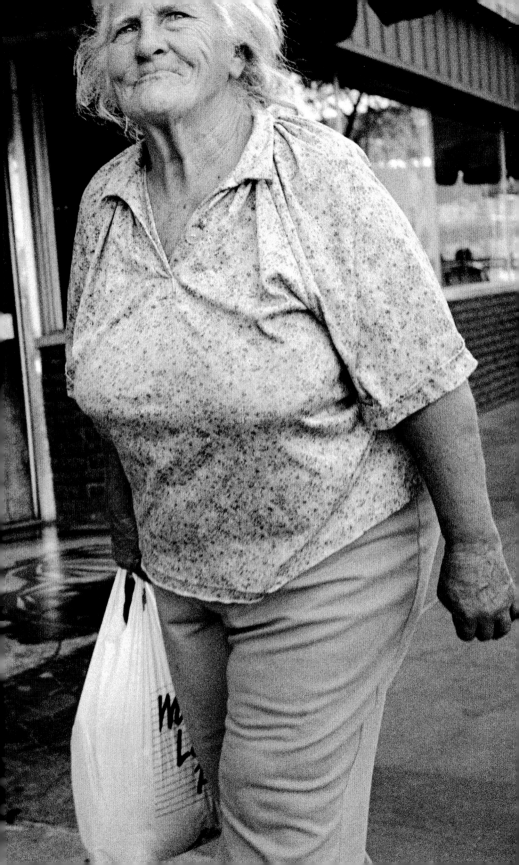

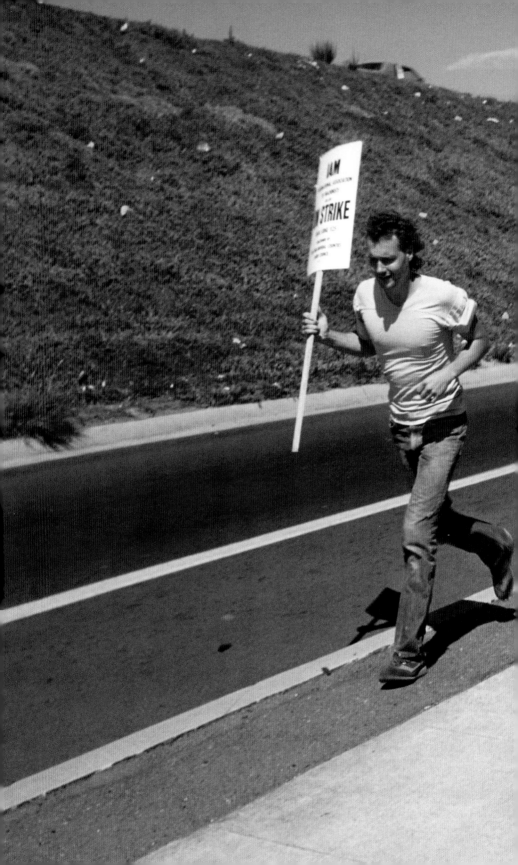

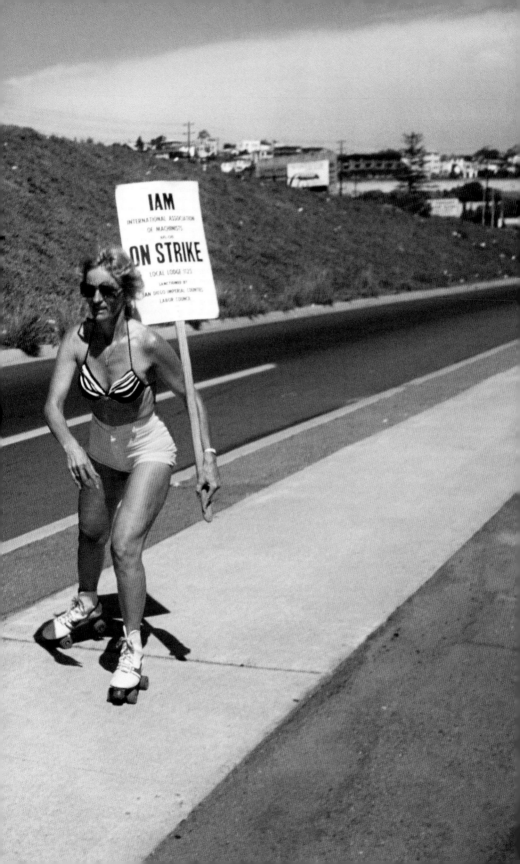

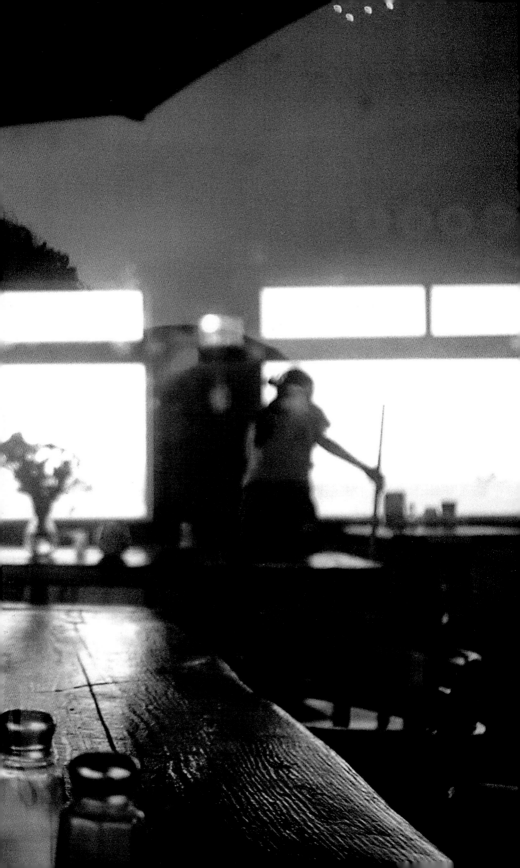

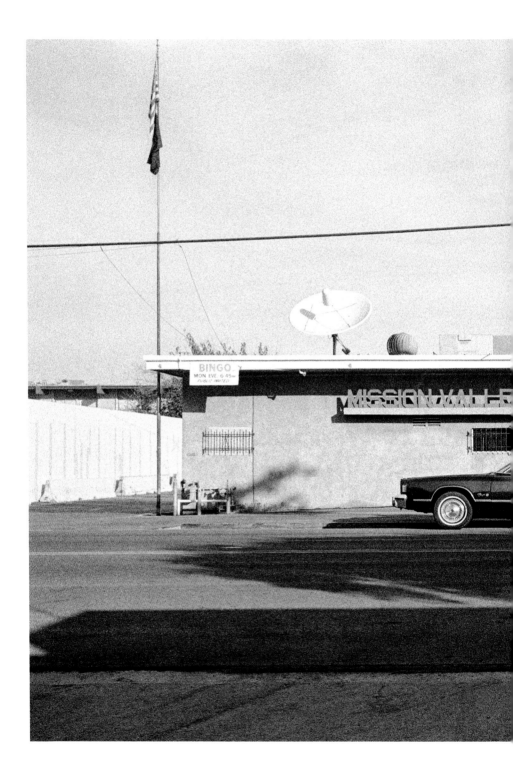

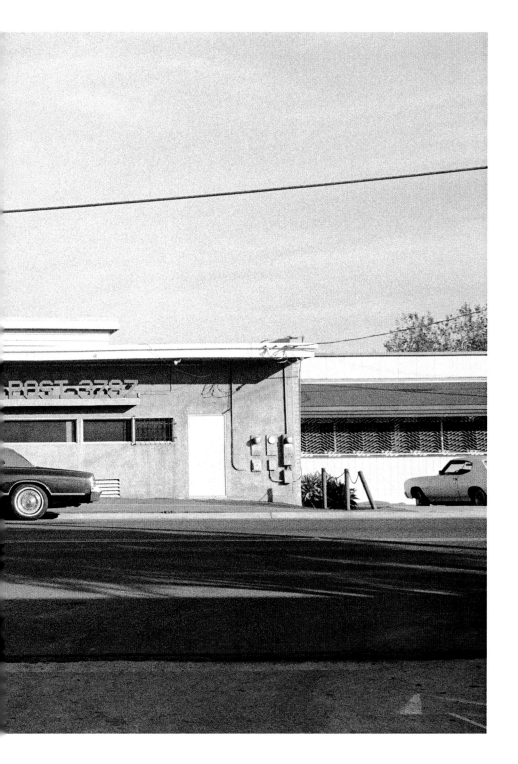

barefoot on the beach with a scarf wrapped around her shoulders, looking out at the horizon and watching the jets rise up from LAX and disappear in the distance.

We hugged and all sat down in the sand together, sharing a big bag of chips we brought along on the bus. Addie started in right away, as if she had little time to loose. "Kip, we grew up together in a pretty bad place, but at least we had some fun. I have to tell you, I wouldn't trade that for anything."

Angie was digging in the wet sand, making mounds between her knees and flattening them out like a bulldozer leveling the ground for a new subdivision.

Addie was sitting with her legs crossed and her back to the wind, fidgety, nervous, strands of loose auburn hair blowing wild across her face. She kept spitting it out of her mouth until she finally tied it back; she seemed a bit high, which was nothing much out the ordinary for my only sister. Her fingers were working overtime, peeling bark from a stick she had picked up in the surf.

"Yeah," I replied, "it's been a bit of a shambles between us. I wish I could have been there more for you. Speaking for myself, it's who I am. I have to accept that 'cause I'm not looking for second chances. I just want to be here with you now, nothing else, really."

"There's something I have to tell you, Kip. I promised Mom I'd never say this, but I have to now 'cause you need to know. She's long gone anyway. When you showed me that old photo of Mom, I saw how you looked at me. I think it's only right for you to know…uh…she's not your mom."

Addie almost stopped breathing and waited a bit to let the words sink in. Her fingers tightened around the stick and it broke in two.

"Huh?"

"She's not your mom, Kip."

All of a sudden I didn't know anything. My mind went blank and everything around me froze like tiny chunks of silver embedded on a strip of film, a still image reversed in the gummy abstraction of a negative. My throat began to tighten. "You're kidding. It's…it's not fair. Why didn't they tell me?"

"I think they didn't want to hurt you any more than they already had. I didn't know myself until she was really dying and she told me her story in detail. She led an extraordinary life but she didn't really think it through, it all just happened. Losing her mom at such an early age didn't give her much confidence, you know?

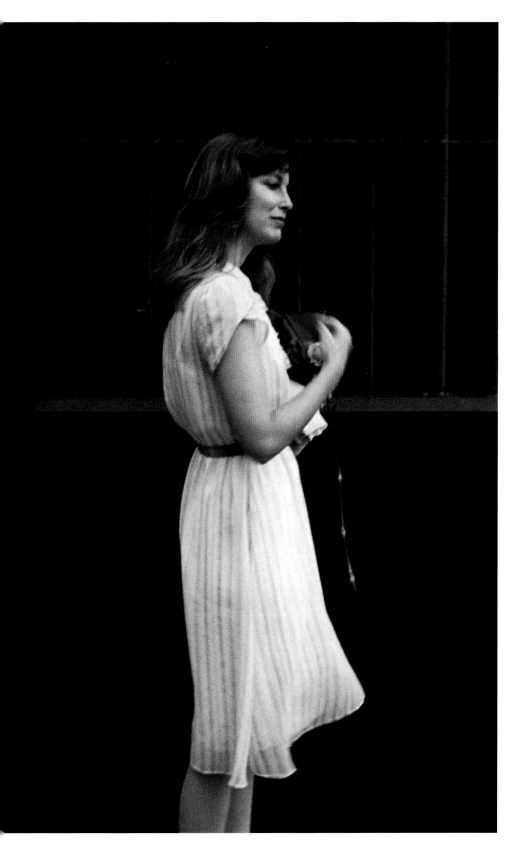

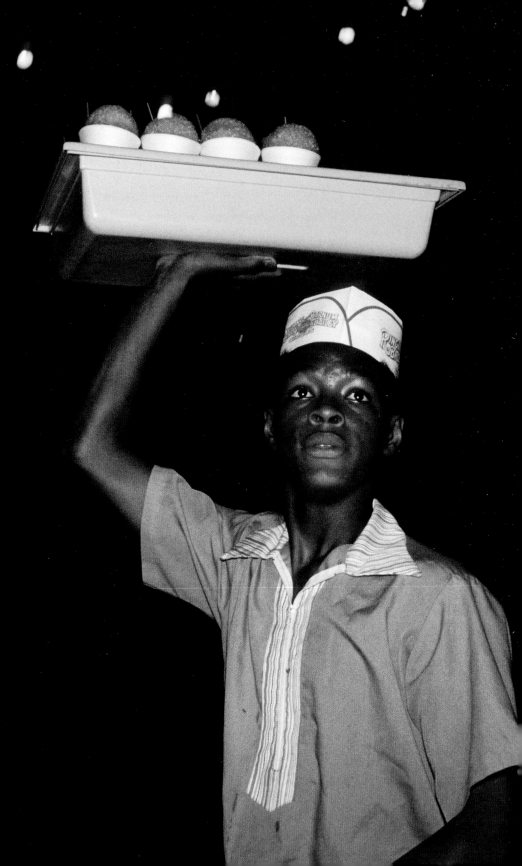

"You lost your mom too, Kip, but that was different. Apparently she abandoned you, left you in the brush out at Muir Beach right after you were born. Somebody found you there. It's lucky you weren't dinner for the seagulls. Mom and Dad heard about it and adopted you 'right off the beach,' so to speak."

Angie sat perfectly still, her eyes glazed over. "Jeez, what a family," she whispered. The ocean air filled her lungs. She listened to her heart pumping blood in a drumbeat that echoed the sound of the waves. "So this means your mom really could be alive, like your dad implied. Probably is. How fucked up is that, Kip?"

"Huh?"

I sat for a long time, almost paralyzed by the first few stars that emerged from twilight, like semaphores signaling code across light-years. Maybe now I knew enough about the past to keep going. "Mom's dead. Jess is gone and buried. I have the snapshot Dad gave me, I have the memories, and that's enough for me."

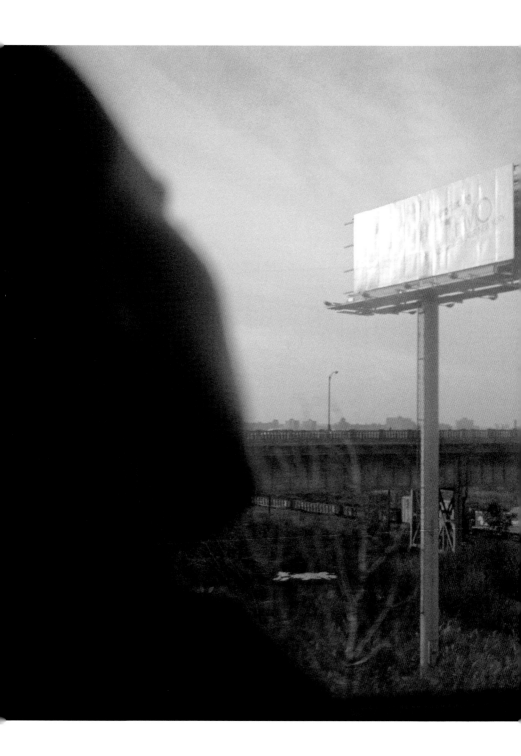

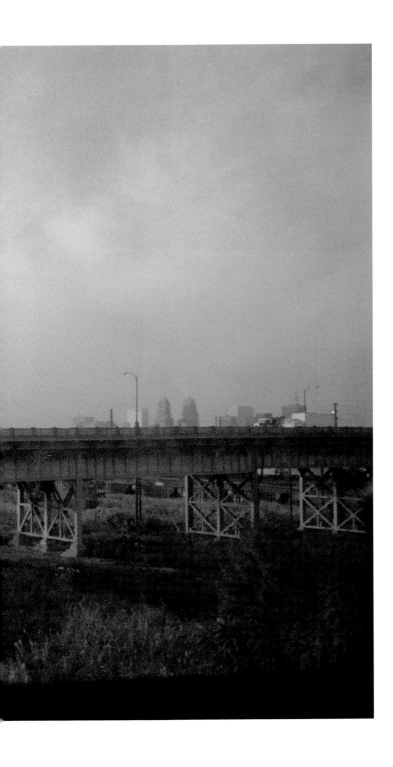

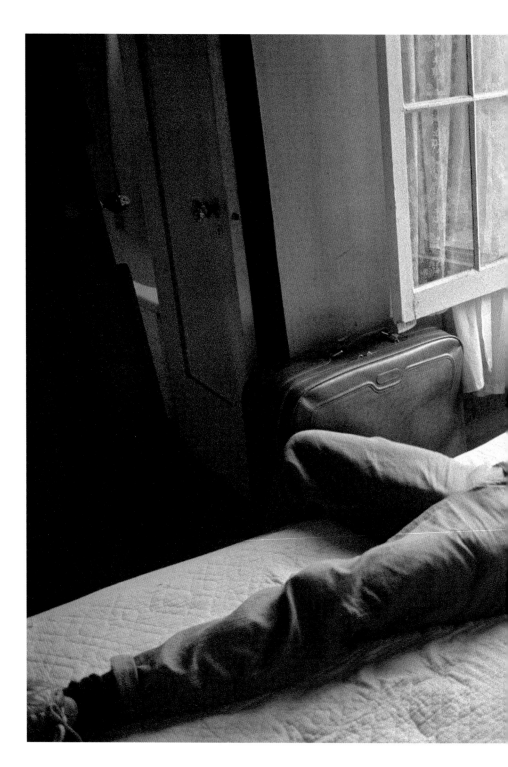

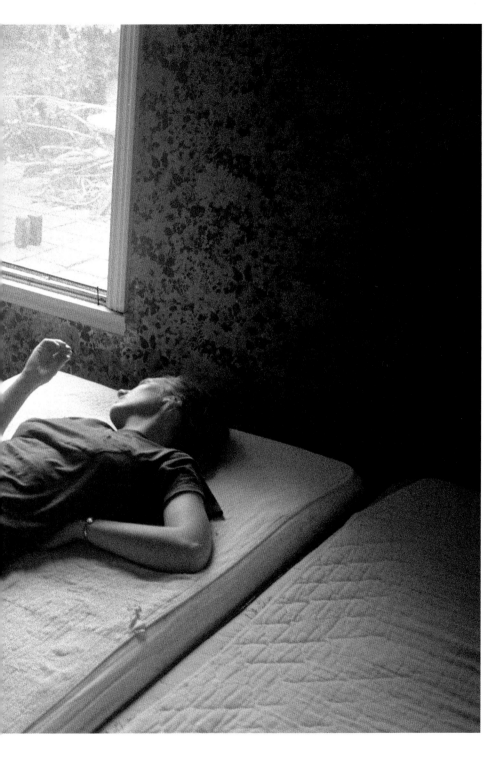

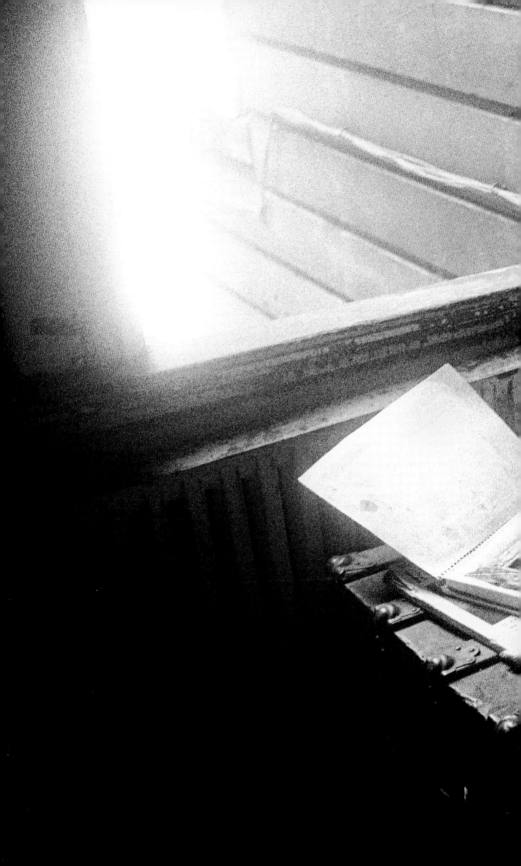

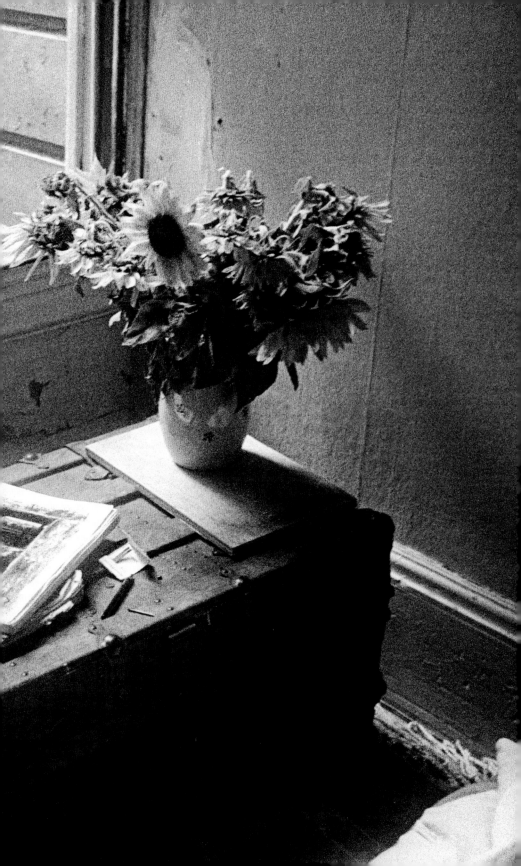

THE IMAGE

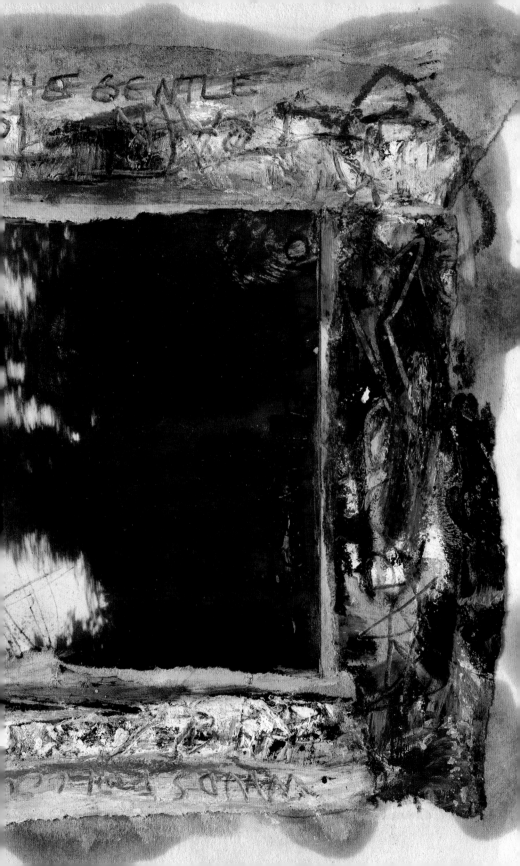

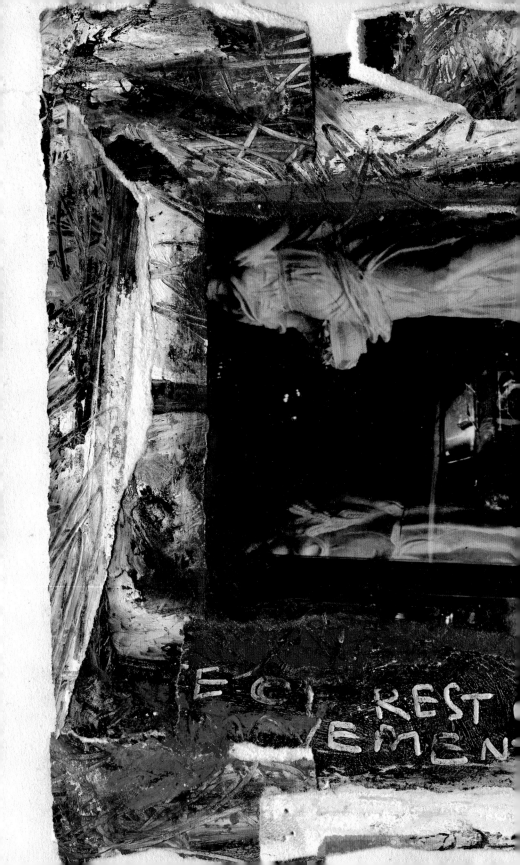

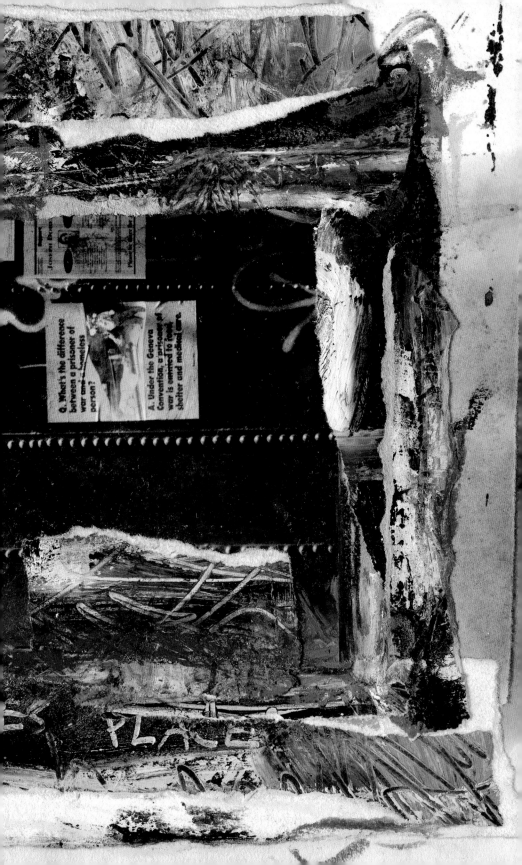

Q. What's the difference between a prisoner of war and a homeless person?

A. Under the Geneva Convention a prisoner of war is entitled to food, shelter and medical care.

PLACE

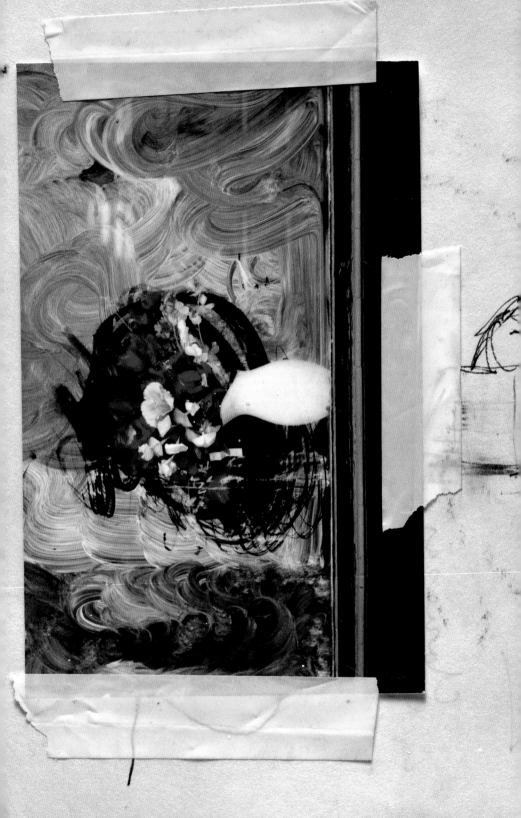

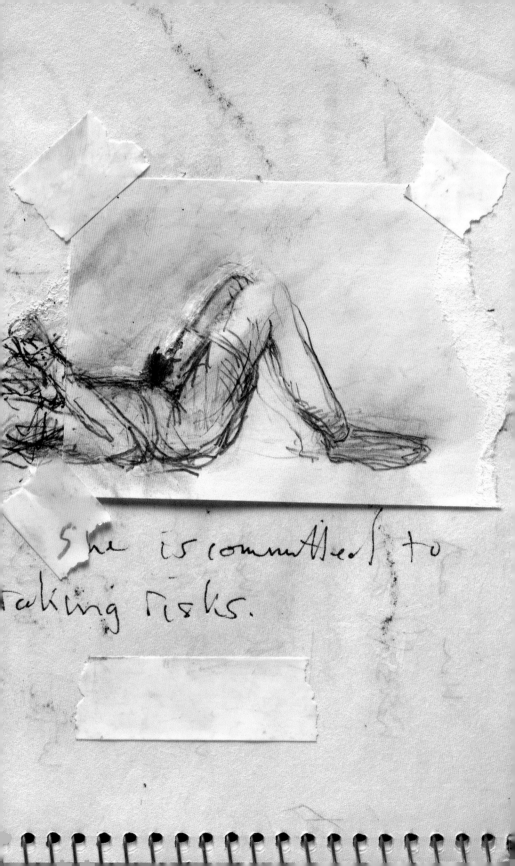

She is committed to
taking risks.

New York City, 1985

When we visited Addie at County General—she OD'd and almost died—she told us not to worry. "This really is a wake-up call and I'm going to be okay. You'll see…."

Two weeks later Angie and I were back in New York, ready to try it again.

"Don't worry, I'm committed this time," she told me during one of our late-night walks to nowhere. We were sitting on the curb at 2 a.m., watching the cabs back up on Bond Street, waiting to turn right down Bowery for an easy after-hours fare. It was cold, and mist clung to the streetlights and made me wish I had brought along something more than an old wool sweater, which was soaking up moisture out of the air like a sponge. The club crowd was shuffling out of CBGB, guys and girls in fashionable black fishnets and leather boots, looking for a ride up or down the Avenues. The growing line of taillights reflected off the pavement, smearing red light across the wet street like the ocean on fire. As the mist turned to a light rain, we decided to head back home, now a small walkup on 11th just off Eighth Avenue.

We were both getting cold, so Angie wrapped her arms around my waist as we made our way down two sets of steps into the subway station at Broadway and Houston. There was always an eerie fluorescent grime that filled the station late at night, a light that bathed everyone in the same green-white glow. The acoustics weren't bad, though, and street musicians and artists liked the place because it was very public. A girl in sweats was practicing classical ballet on the platform, stretching her arms high over her head, turning, bending in slow, graceful movements, then a leap and pirouette, all in perfect time with the baroque sounds of Mozart coming from a boombox she had set down on the platform edge alongside a cup with a three quarters and a dime inside. A few other late-night types stopped to watch, and by the time the deafening sound of an approaching express rattled through the station, she was well into a short dance routine from *Ideomeno*. The decibel level in the station rose up about a million times, drowning out Mozart, then dissipated as the train shot through the tunnel.

Dressed for a night out, an old woman turned to her husband, mouthing something he couldn't hear. He cupped his hand to his ear and leaned in close as she shouted over the racket, "I'm telling you, I could watch that show again."

We walked down toward the end of the platform, a move that would put us in the right car for a fast exit at West 4th. Four punks—eighteen, maybe nineteen years old, and together as much for protection as friendship—huddled in the shadows. The tallest one was still wired, pacing back and forth, but he was starting to ease out of his day. "Breakfast is okay there," he explained to the others. "But since I'm never up before two, I get the grilled cheese from the lunch menu. It doesn't cost much at all, maybe two and some change."

"Yeah right," said his friend, a skinhead who was tougher and looked wasted, semi-buff in tight black jeans and a faded T with the arms cut off to expose a tattoo of a green and red sea serpent winding up his arm toward his neck. He was kneeling on the platform edge, looking down the tracks for the F train. "Like I care what you're gonna have for breakfast. You better save your money or you'll be hurtin' like me. Where's the fuckin' F? I'm gonna pass out right here."

"Well, I'm not eatin' no grilled cheese," said the lone girl in the group with a loopy island accent; she was tall and dark with frizzy hair, a loose pink tank top, and a brush sticking out of her hip pocket. "Strawberry yogurt, that's what I want. I'm going for a real magazine look, you know, the innocent fashion warrior, like that chick Sarah-what's-her-face in *The Terminator*." She raised her arms overhead imitating the ballerina and spun around, tossing a couple of awkward kung fu jabs toward the snake man, shadow boxing him just to keep moving. He was zoned out as she approached him from behind; she eased her hands up over both his ears and pulled his head back gently like she was going to kiss him on the lips.

Everyone was laughing as we inched closer for a better look. Then she squeezed her hands together hard, putting uncomfortable pressure on his ears, and pulled him backward till he lost balance. "You're terminated, fucker," she snarled to spotty applause from the group, as the F local careered into the station with a clatter that drowned out the moment.

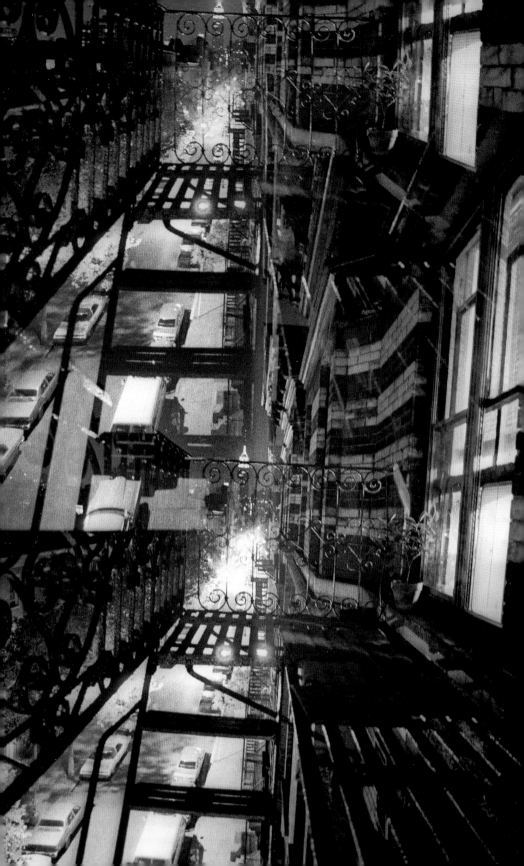

Images

Jacket. *Watsonville, Red Dress*, 1982; **4–5.** *Inside Passage*, 1928; **6.** *Horoscope*, 1975; **7.** *Immigration*, date unknown; **8.** *Oaxaca*, 1948; **11.** *California 1969*, 1955; **12–13.** *Postcard*, 1985; **14–15.** *San Anselmo, Kodak Film*, 1970; **17.** *Tomales, Boy by the Pier*, 1969; **18–19.** *Mexico City, Dancing in the Park*, 2002; **20–21.** *Mexico City, Día de los Muertos*, 2002; **22.** *Guaymas, Two Girls*, 1971; **24–25.** *Oaxaca, Dead Horse*, 1948; **26–27.** *Santa Cruz, Yellow Tree*, 1976; **30–31.** *Santa Cruz, Radar on the Rug*, 1978; **32–33.** *Santa Cruz, Flowering Tree*, 1977; **34–35.** *Santa Cruz, Girl Playing*, 1976; **36–37.** *Watsonville, Rail Yard*, 1982; **40–41.** *Santa Cruz, Moosehead Beer*, 1981; **42–43.** *Santa Cruz, Afro*, 1981; **45.** *Santa Cruz, Bow Tie*, 1981; **50–51.** *Santa Cruz, Boy on the Beach*, 1977; **53.** *San Diego, Big Gulp*, 1984; **54–55.** *San Francisco, Sportsman*, 1980; **57.** *Santa Cruz, Theater Manager*, 1981; **58–59.** *Redondo Beach, Judy*, 1983; **60–61.** *Los Angeles, Motel*, 1975; **64–65.** *San Diego, Preacher, Balboa Park*, 1983; **66.** *San Francisco, Barbecue*, 1993; **70–71.** *Santa Cruz, Sailboat*, 1978; **72–73.** *Santa Cruz, Two Girls*, 1981; **74–75.** *Watsonville, Cannery Outlet*, 1982; **79.** *Santa Cruz, Girl in the Light*, 1978; **81.** *San Diego, Man in Green Cap*, 1984; **82–83.** *San Francisco, Homeless Woman*, 1990; **85.** *Oakland, Boys Playing*, 1994; **86–87.** *Watsonville, Magazine*, 1982; **88–89.** *San Francisco, Kids on the Car*, 1972; **90.** *Santa Cruz, Vin Rose*, 1981; **91.** *Santa Cruz, Old Man*, 1981; **92–93.** *Santa Cruz, Beach Flats*, 1981; **96.** *New York City, TV*, 1985; **97.** *Santa Cruz, Missionary Girl*, 1981; **98–99.** *Capitola, Nixon Resigns*, 1974; **103.** *El Paso, Palm Sunday*, 1983; **104–105.** *San Diego, Juan Correa's Family Album*, 1988; **106–107.** *Watsonville, Baton*, 1982; **108–109.** *Watsonville, Strawberry Workers*, 1982; **110–111.** *Watsonville, Girl with New Boots*, 1982; **112–113.** *Salinas, Rodeo Grounds*, 1983; **114.** *Watsonville, Cannery Worker*, 1982; **115.** *Watsonville, Sisters*, 1982; **116–117.** *Watsonville, Radiator Works*, 1982; **118–119.** *Childhood Memories*, 1990; **122–123.** *San Juan Bautista, U.S. 101 South*, 1981; **124–125.** *Light of Memory*, 2012; **128–129.** *San Juan Bautista, Grave*, 1981; **130.** *Lewiston, Betty Jo*, 1936; **132–133.** *Delaware Memorial Bridge, U.S. 40*, 1995; **136–137.** *New York City, Subway*, 1977; **138–139.** *New York City, Avenue A*, 1977; **140–141.** *New York City, Sullivan Street*, 1975; **144–145.** *New York City, Central Park, Summer*, 1978; **146–147.** *New York City, Guernica*, 1978; **148–149.** *New York City, Canal Street, Winter*, 1978; **150–151.** *New York City, 9 Eldridge Street*, 2012;

Acknowledgments

Although this is a work of fiction, I have always used photography like a diary, making images that document people and places, as well as the more intangible things, like memories, impressions, and feelings. *Redlands* is drawn from these diaries, experiences, and ideas. It brings together the insights and assistance of all my family, friends, and colleagues.

Jim Goldberg was my collaborator on this book. He pushed me to make it better.

David Avalos, Eduardo Carrillo, Richard Diebenkorn, Veronique Enrique, Robert Frank, Guillermo Gómez-Peña, Sarah Greenough, June Leaf, Martha Orendorff, Gordon Parks, Gilles Peress, Sandra Phillips, Jock Reynolds, Nan Rosenthal, Kippy Stroud, Larry Sultan, Anne Tucker, and Donald Weygandt all helped me to understand words and pictures in new ways.

I am also grateful to the following people, whose ongoing encouragement and support helped make *Redlands* possible: Norman Carr, John Cohen, Salvador Güereña, Mark Gulezian, Betsy Karel, Michael Mack, Joe Mills, Paul Roth, and Mark Swartz.

Colección Tloque Nahuaque, Davidson Library, University of California, Santa Barbara; Epson America, Inc.; Kyocera Yashica Corporation; and Special Collections, McHenry Library, University of California, Santa Cruz each helped facilitate research, donated equipment, or provided technical assistance for this project.

I am truly indebted to Gerhard Steidl for believing in my work, following my progress, publishing *Redlands*, and sharing it with the world. He provided the insight, expertise, and boundless creative and technical resources that were needed to realize this book. My thanks also goes to the fine staff at Steidl Verlag, Göttingen, especially Bernard Fischer, Sabine Hahn, Maren Mittentzwey, Rudi Schellong, Moritz Scheper, and Inès Schumann.

Redlands is dedicated to my family: Amy and Daniel Brookman, who gave me the inspiration, courage, support, and time to do something new; my parents, Marjorie and Bernard Brookman, who got me my first cameras and encouraged my dreams; my grandparents, Sophie and Herman Brookman, who would never talk about their roots but gave me the old Leica; and Austin and Elizabeth Kilian, who fought hard to encourage creative thinking.

Philip Brookman
Göttingen, February 2015

Book design: Philip Brookman, Bernard Fischer, and Gerhard Steidl
Separations: Steidl's digital darkroom
Production and printing: Steidl, Göttingen

Steidl
Düstere Str. 4 / 37073 Göttingen, Germany
Phone +49 551 49 60 60 / Fax +49 551 49 60 649
mail@steidl.de
steidl.de

ISBN 978-3-86930-686-5
Printed in Germany by Steidl